THE CHURCH PLANTER'S HANDBOOK

*God Bless
in His Service*

T·H·E
CHURCH
PLANTER'S
HANDBOOK

Larry L. Lewis

BROADMAN PRESS

NASHVILLE, TENNESSEE

4260-68

ISBN: 0-8054-6068-3
Library of Congress Card Catalog Number: 92-25513
Printed in the United States of America

All Scripture quotations are from the *King James Version*.

Library of Congress Cataloging-in-Publication Data

Lewis, Larry L.
    The church planter's handbook / Larry L. Lewis.
      p. cm.
    Includes bibliographical references.
    ISBN 0-8054-6068-3
    1. Church development, New.   I. Title.
  BV652.24.L48   1992
  254′.1—dc20   92-25513
                                               CIP

DEDICATION

This book is dedicated to a man I never met or knew but whose shadow hovers over me. He is my great-grandfather, Marcellus Whiteside, a late-nineteenth-century church planter who reportedly started over forty Baptist churches in Missouri. Perhaps I inherited my church-planter heart from this good man. He was a true biblical "tentmaker," making his own way as a bivocational farmer/ preacher, and was probably against the whole idea of mission boards. I admire him greatly and when I meet him someday in heaven, we're going to have a good long chat about starting churches.

CONTENTS

INTRODUCTION

"God's plan to win America to Christ is to sow this nation down with Bible-preaching, soul-winning churches."

I heard this statement in 1961, shortly after I had gone to Columbus, Ohio, to be the mission pastor of the newly founded Parsons Baptist Church. The speaker was Dr. Ray Roberts, executive director of the State Convention of Baptists in Ohio, and a Southern Baptist pioneer in home mission work in the Northeast.

I believe even more strongly today that God's plan not only to evangelize the nation but to minister to the needs of people everywhere is through the establishment of loving, caring, witnessing, ministering churches. Everywhere there are people, regardless of their racial, ethnic, or socioeconomic background, there needs to be a church in the midst of them, ministering to their needs and proclaiming the gospel of Christ.

I first felt God's call to the ministry while a high school student in Missouri. Shortly after my graduation, I was licensed to preach and pastored my first country church at eighteen years of age. A year later I was called to the Hopewell Baptist Church at Thompson, Missouri. Our church was located only a few miles from the country rest home, sometimes called the "poor farm." I realized no matter how hard we tried, most of the people within the four walls of that huge building would never attend our services, would never hear the gospel we preached every Sunday, or would ever experience the benefits of our ministry. The only way to reach them would be to take the gospel to them, penetrating their "cluster" with witness and ministry.

I spoke with the management, and they willingly agreed for our church to conduct services at the county farm every Sunday afternoon. From that point on, we conducted worship services in the lounge areas upstairs and downstairs with a total attendance of forty to fifty people. We visited every bedfast patient, reading a few verses of Scripture and having prayer.

In doing so, we penetrated an "ethnae," a people group that would not have otherwise been reached, establishing an "indigenous, satellite unit" with meaningful witness and ministry.

God richly blessed! Numbers of residents of the county farm came to know Jesus as Savior and found new life and hope from our weekly visits.

Instead of preaching four times every Sunday, twice at the mother church and twice at the county farm, I would have been wise to have assigned that ministry to a good, godly layperson. In my spiritual immaturity I perceived that only I, the pastor, was duly qualified to lead this ministry. How foolish to believe that God will not raise up and equip members of the body for this type of outreach task.

Nevertheless, a meaningful, fruitful mission ministry was established with congregational singing, Bible preaching, a clear presentation of the gospel, and genuine, Spirit-filled worship, although this might not be considered a "church-type mission" in the traditional sense of the word.

Most important, it enabled our little country church to fulfill our Lord's clear command in Mark 16:15, "Go ye into all the world and preach the gospel to *every* creature" (emphasis added). To be true to that command, we must penetrate all "clusters" of people wherever they may be with a clear gospel witness. Total penetration of every community with the gospel must be our objective and total participation of all members of the body must be our goal![1]

While I was a student at Southwestern Baptist Theological Seminary in Fort Worth, Texas, I began to sense the call of the "apostle." As I explain in chapter 5, I believe with deep conviction that the biblical call of the apostle referred to in Ephesians

4:11 is the call to be a church planter. I sensed this call just as surely as I had earlier sensed the call to preach and to the ministry. Although I admired the pastors of large churches with great buildings, large budgets, and many members, I did not sense that as God's will for my life.

I had deep concern for foreign missions, led the churches I pastored to give generously to world mission causes, and deeply appreciated those serving on the foreign mission field. Again, I did not sense this was God's will for me.

Rather, I sensed very clearly the Lord would have me go to that place in our own United States where there was no church but where a church was needed and begin a new work. I knew the work would be hard and the reward would be small. I realized there would be many problems and frustrations, but I could think of nothing more exciting than beginning a new church and seeing it grow to become a strong, self-supporting lighthouse for God.

During a missions service at Southwestern Seminary, I walked forward to the front of Truett Auditorium, submitting to what I sensed to be the call of the apostle in my life, committing myself to the challenge of being a church planter. Shortly after graduation, opportunity knocked at my door!

A new mission had started in Columbus, Ohio, meeting in the Parsons Elementary School. They invited me to come in view of a call as the mission pastor. I preached to the congregation of sixteen members in the school building on Sunday morning, then met with that same congregation Sunday evening in the living room of one of the members. During that Sunday evening service, I challenged them, if they called me as pastor, to set a goal to have one thousand enrolled in Sunday School within five years, to have at least five hundred in attendance, and to start at least one new mission every year. Even though they were only sixteen members strong, they were excited by these goals and called me as their pastor.

We continued to meet in the elementary school for three years until we had purchased a site and built a lovely new building. By the end of five years, we did not have the one thousand enrolled or five hundred attendance that we had envisioned, but we did have more than eight hundred enrolled and were consistently averaging over four hundred in attendance. We were successful in reaching our goal of starting a new mission every year. We never felt it hindered us, hampered us, or hurt us to be "tithing our membership" annually, taking some of our finest members to be the nucleus of a new work we were establishing in a needed area.

After having served five years in Columbus, I sensed God's apostolic call to another area of the Northeast. The Delaware Valley Baptist Church in Willingboro, New Jersey, was the first Southern Baptist church in the Greater Philadelphia area. It was in a sea of new homes comprising what was originally called Levittown, New Jersey, a planned-community suburb of Philadelphia. In the midst of this rapidly growing suburban community, Southern Baptists had a small church meeting in the basement of a house. They were averaging about sixty in attendance and had already filled the building to capacity.

During my first meeting with them, I challenged them with three goals—have one thousand enrolled in Sunday School with an average of five hundred in attendance by the end of five years and start at least one new mission every year. (Sounds familiar, doesn't it?)

God blessed and the church grew rapidly. In order to accommodate additional Sunday School classes and departments and the rapidly increasing attendance, we utilized nearby buildings, homes, and even school buses. The entire children's division met for both Sunday School and worship at the Country Ridge Elementary School. The youth division met for Sunday School at the Garfield Elementary School, then were transported to the church for worship. Several Sunday School departments and classes met on "double-duty" church buses which were used to transport riders to Sunday School and worship but were also used for Sunday School departments and classes. We conducted four worship services every Sunday filled to capacity, averaging more than three hundred in attendance and meeting in a house that was built to accommodate a family of four or five people. In spite of this rapid growth, we did not reach our goal of one thousand enrolled, but we did have more than seven hundred. Neither did we reach our goal of five hundred in attendance at the end of five years, but were consistently averaging about three hundred fifty. Nevertheless, we did achieve our goal of starting a new mission every year. Again, we never felt it hurt us to be taking members to become the nucleus of a new work. Rather, we felt we were all the more blessed for it and that this was one of the reasons for our rapid growth. At that time, Delaware Valley Baptist Church had experienced the fastest growth and was the largest Anglo Southern Baptist church in the Northeast.

When the Baptist Convention of Pennsylvania-South Jersey was formed in 1970, I was asked to be the director of religious education. I had a significant role in forming the new convention, having served on the steering committee of the Pennsylvania-South Jersey Fellowship for several years and then on the executive committee of the new convention when it was first constituted. I was chairman of the search committee that employed the first executive director. He, along with the state convention personnel committee, asked me to be the director of religious education; the two of us along with two secretaries composing the entire staff.

Here again, I was able to exercise my apostolic function as a church planter. Most of my time was given to helping establish new churches, train their workers, and organize their program of work. During the almost four years I served on the state staff, we saw over one hundred new churches established throughout Pennsylvania and southern New Jersey.

After serving fourteen years as a church planter and mission pastor in the Northeast, I was called as pastor of the Tower Grove Baptist Church in St. Louis, Missouri. What a change after fourteen years on the pioneer field working with new, struggling congregations! Tower Grove was a church with several thousand members in midtown St. Louis. At one time, Tower Grove had been one of the fastest growing churches in the nation, leading the Southern Baptist Convention in baptisms. However, as is the case with many churches in a transitional community, the church had suffered decline for many years. From 1962 to 1971 the church declined in attendance from 1,953 to 716. During my predecessor's two-year tenure, attendance had turned around and was beginning to grow again, However, with the prevalence of community transition, racial change, and socioeconomic change, every forward step was difficult.

During my seven years at Tower Grove, we integrated our congregation, established a multiministry program that was church-based, Christ-centered, and redemptive in every respect. The church led the state of Missouri in baptisms each year, averaging more than two hundred, and attendance grew from 844 to over twelve hundred.

However, I feel our greatest opportunity for growth was completely neglected. I put aside my goal, adhered to so faithfully in Ohio and New Jersey, of starting a new mission every year. I was totally deluded by the prevalent perception that there were already too many churches in St. Louis, that most of the churches in the city were declining, and we certainly didn't need to start any more.

Like most of my fellow pastors, the idea of starting new congregations that would meet the need of the changing community had escaped me. Although Tower Grove was making some progress in reaching people of other than Anglo background, compared to the black and ethnic population, our success was minuscule.

It wasn't until I had pastored Tower Grove several years that I became acquainted with the "homogeneous unit principle." I became convinced that the only, truly effective approach to evangelizing and congregationalizing people of other races, backgrounds, and culture was to establish congregations homogeneously in sync with their own backgrounds. Although every church must not only welcome but aggressively seek to evangelize and enlist all people, regardless of their race, ethnicity, or socioeconomic status, in most cases more will be reached by extension than will be reached by expansion. In the transitional community, the church will likely grow far more by starting new congregations than simply continuing to enlarge the mother church.

We discovered a church building for sale just a few blocks north of the Tower Grove facility but in the midst of a predominantly African-American community. The little Anglo congregation that had met there for many years had dwindled to about ten people and finally decided to merge with a suburban church of the same denomination. They offered us the building and all the equipment for a total of $5,000! What a godsend! We called a young black pastor, a recent graduate of one of our seminaries, and the first Sunday there were more than one hundred in attendance! A fine black congregation exists there today as a vital, viable witness to that community.

I am convinced this same experience could have been multiplied many times throughout downtown and midtown St. Louis had we only had the vision of multiple congregations.

"Coloring outside the lines" is now the norm in Southern Baptist church planting. Literally thousands of Southern Baptist congregations meet in community rooms, lodge halls, school buildings, Seventh-Day Adventist buildings, Jewish synagogues, living rooms or basements of someone's home, mobile chapels, motel or hotel conference rooms, funeral parlors, and some even meet outside in the open air.

In a few short years Southern Baptists have changed from being a very colloquial, parochial denomination, located mostly in the South and made up of predominantly white, Anglo, English-speaking Southerners. Today, the Southern Baptist Convention has churches in every state of the Union, plus the territories of Puerto Rico, American Samoa, Guam, and the Virgin Islands. Also, Southern Baptists have churches throughout Canada. More than 6,000 of our 43,000 congregations are now ethnic, with worship services and Bible teaching conducted every week in 103 different languages! We now rejoice to have more than 1,500 predominantly black Baptist congregations affiliated with the Southern Baptist Convention.

Even so, we have merely "touched the hem of the garment." State directors of missions in our 41 Southern Baptist state conventions have already identified 22,000 places where new churches need to be started immediately! There are probably at least twice that many more that have not yet been identified. Of course, many will be in ethnic areas where we are seeking to evangelize and congregationalize the more than five hundred different language groups in America today, and in the vast predominantly black communities, especially of our great metropolitan areas.

From 65 to 80 percent of those living in the central cities of America reside in multifamily housing. These represent the largest group of unevangelized, unchurched people in the nation. Fewer churches per population are found in the inner cities and mid cities than anywhere else.

English-speaking Anglos still remain the vast majority of the population in America today. According to the 1990 census, 75.6 percent of America's population is Anglo. Nearly every city has burgeoning suburbs with hundreds of thousands of new homes being built every year. As a new suburban community is formed, new congregations need to be formed there also. If it's important for those people to have a shopping center nearby, a service station to service their automobiles, or school buildings in which to educate their children, it is equally important there be a Bible-teaching, soul-winning, ministering church there also. As they lay out that new suburb, let's be there laying out a new congregation.

My prayer is that this book may prove helpful as you seek to be an instrument in God's hand doing what I believe is the most important work in the world, establishing new churches where new churches are needed. God bless you in this important task.

NOTE

1. Darrell Robinson, *Total Church Life*, (Nashville: Broadman Press, 1991), 7-18.

1

FORESIGHT

"Where there is no vision, the people perish" (Prov. 29:18).

Southern Baptists have set some ambitious and challenging goals to direct us as we approach the year A.D. 2000. One of the most challenging of these is "50,000 by 2000," the goal to have 50,000 Southern Baptist congregations (that is, constituted churches and church-type missions), by the end of this century. To accomplish this goal, Southern Baptists will need a minimum of 1,200 church starts a year, allowing for the defection of numbers of churches every year in the denomination that either die, merge with another church, affiliate with another denomination, or become independent. To net an increase of two congregations, we have to start at least three.

In March 1991, Dr. Charles Chaney, vice-president of extension for the Home Mission Board of the Southern Baptist Convention, spoke to a meeting of state church extension directors in Chicago, Illinois. He explained to the directors that for several years Southern Baptists have been starting more than three churches a day and challenged them to increase that number to four. As a result, the "15,000 Campaign" was launched, an effort to start 15,000 new Southern Baptist churches by the end of the year 2000. That is 1,500 church starts per year for ten years, or approximately four per day. This is more churches than Southern Baptists, perhaps more than any other denomination, have ever started in any one decade. What a challenge!

However, the reason we start new churches throughout America and around the world is not to reach a denominational goal or to fulfill some denominational program. Goals are to direct us, not drive us. Achieving goals is never an end in itself. No church should ever be started just to meet a numerical goal, either from the denomination, a state convention, a local association, or even a goal set by the church itself. Only as God Himself clearly and specifically leads and a specific area of need is identified should new congregations be planted.

The real goal is not to have 50,000 congregations by the year 2000 or 1,500 new church starts per year. Our ultimate goal is to evangelize and congregationalize America. Our purpose is to fulfill the Great Commission by establishing Bible-preaching, soul-winning, ministering churches everywhere there are people.

Every pastor must seek a vision from the Lord as to where new congregations need to be established in his area. It may be a new suburban community where a new church needs to be established with the expectation it will soon be indigenous and self-supporting. It may be a government housing project or a high-rise apartment. It may be a transitional community where large numbers of blacks are moving in and whites are moving out. It may be an ethnic area where a large number of people of some other language or background are not effectively being reached by any church.

The incentive for starting a new work comes with a heavy burden for the lost and a direct vision from God of a need to be fulfilled and an opportunity to be met. The Bible says, "Except there be a vision, the people perish." If some pastor and some church does not see the vision for establishing a new work in that community, the people there will perish in their sins and be doomed and dammed to hell forever. Likewise, if the church itself does not have a mission vision, it will likely perish even in the midst of thousands of people waiting to be reached for Christ.

In his excellent book, *Church Planting for a Greater Harvest,* Peter Wagner sees church planting as essential to effective evangelism. He states, "The single most effective evangelistic methodology under heaven is planting new churches." He goes on to say, "Without exception the growing denominations have been those who have stressed church planting."

Wagner uses Southern Baptists as an example of a denomination that has grown primarily as a result of its strong emphasis on church extension.

It is not by accident that Southern Baptists have become the largest Protestant denomination in America. One of their secrets is that they constantly invest substantial resources of personnel and finances in church planting on all levels from the local congregations to associations to state conventions to their Home Mission Board in Atlanta. Much of what I have learned about church planting I have learned from Southern Baptists.

Wagner gives five reasons why he feels planting new churches is so important:

1. Church planting is biblical. Church planting is the New Testament way of extending the gospel.

2. Church planting means denominational survival. One of the absolutely essential ingredients for reversing the decline (in many denominations) is vigorously planting new churches.

3. Church planting develops new leadership. New churches open wide the doors of leadership and ministry challenges and the entire body of Christ subsequently benefits.

4. Church planting stimulates existing churches. In more cases than not, a new church in the community tends to raise the religious interest of the people in general and, if handled properly, can be of benefit to existing churches. That which blesses the Kingdom of God as a whole, also blesses the churches that truly are a part of the Kingdom.

5. Church planting is efficient. There is no more practical or cost-effective way of bringing unbelievers to Christ in a given geographical area than planting new churches.[1]

Most of us are familiar with that Scripture in Matthew 28:19-20 called the "Great Commission." In His last words to the disciples, Jesus said, "Go ye therefore, and teach [disciple] all nations [ethnaes], baptizing them in the name of the Father, and of the Son, and of the Holy Ghost: Teaching them to observe all things whatsoever I have commanded you.'' What did Jesus mean when He commanded, ''disciple all nations''?

The Greek word for nation is *ethnae* from which we derive the word *ethnic*. Literally, He was commanding that we not only disciple and baptize all nations of the world, but all nationalities. In the United States alone there are more than five hundred language groups. Thanks be to God, Southern Baptists now have congregations ministering to more than one hundred of these groups.

However, there is much yet to be done if we are serious about fulfilling our mandate from the Lord to evangelize and congregationalize all language groups. Literally thousands of ethnic churches must be started throughout America, especially in the large cities, if we are truly Great Commission Christians. Most of these new ethnic congregations will not have the resources necessary to buy land, build a building, or hire a full-time pastor. Many, if not most, will have to be started and continue in temporary facilities led by bivocational pastors and volunteers. Nevertheless, these congregations must be started and this work must be done if we are serious about fulfilling the Great Commission in our day and in our nation.

Some have translated the Greek word *ethnae* as ''people groups.'' This is a true and accurate translation, for many times great cultures of people transcend all national and political boundaries. For example, the Jews are a people group that can only be reached effectively within their own heritage and culture, but they transcend many national boundaries. People groups must be reached in a manner consistent with their culture and heritage without, in any way, compromising the gospel we proclaim. Messianic fellowships are great examples of contextual evangelism.

Dr. Rex Lindsay, executive director of the Kansas-Nebraska Convention of Southern Baptists, has defined the word *ethnae* as ''swarm'' or ''cluster.'' He likens it to a swarm of bees that gather together in their own intricate, well-organized society. Every bee knows its own swarm and, no matter where it journeys, it will return to its own home. It does not get confused and return to the wrong hive. The swarm has its own queen and a very sophisticated social order. They communicate in their own language and in their own way. No matter how eloquent and powerful of speech a human may be, he will not do well communicating with a bee unless he is one of them and part of their swarm.

In the Great Commission Jesus reminds us that our world is filled with ''people swarms''—clusters of people with their own history, heritage, traditions, culture, language, values, philosophies, and belief systems. If we are to be effective in evangelizing and congregationalizing these clusters, we must penetrate the swarm. The apostle Paul declared, ''I am made all things to all men that I might by all means save some'' (1 Cor. 9:22). This is certainly chapter and verse sufficient for contextual evangelism and church planting. Without compromising the gospel in any way, we must do the same.

Much diversity exists in America even among English-speaking Anglos. Social patterns, cultural backgrounds, economic status, educational levels, and life-style choices group people in today's society. These ''people characteristics'' must be recognized and respected. New churches are needed that penetrate all people groups in society.

First Baptist Church, Arlington, Texas, has done a magnificent job of penetrating the ''swarms'' in the Greater Arlington area. They now have more than one hundred mission congregations, most of them led by lay people from the church congregation, meeting weekly for Bible study, prayer, worship, and preaching. They gather in meeting rooms of apartment buildings and other temporary facilities. Their total attendance averages well over one thousand every week, nearly as many as the mother church itself. But even while starting over one hundred mission congregations, the mother church has grown from approximately twelve hundred in average attendance to more than sixteen hundred in only five years. This proves once again that it does not hurt a church to start new missions, but rather usually enhances its own growth as well.

Jesus said, "Give, and it shall be given unto you; good measure, pressed down, and shaken together, and running over" (Luke 6:38). Do you believe that promise applies to a church as well as to an individual Christian? Is it possible to outgive God? Doesn't this promise imply that the church that gives itself in mission support will profit by doing so?

Leading the church to tithe its membership as well as its resources, giving even of its finest members as well as sacrificially from its budget so that new congregations can be established where they are needed, is a source of great blessing to the mother congregation. Members give more generously of their resources and are more enthusiastic in their support for the church when they perceive their church to be strongly committed to missions and church planting. In fact, the most counterproductive thing any church can do to meet a financial crisis, it to cut back on mission support. To do so signals to the congregation that missions and mission support is not a priority.

In his address to state convention mission leaders in Chicago, Dr. Charles Chaney cited five reasons why new churches need to be started:

I. *Our Constant Obligation to the Lord.* The Research Department of the Home Mission Board estimates that 172,000,000 people in the United States have never personally accepted Christ. There are only four nations in the world, besides the United States, that have a total population of 172 million. This country is one of the great mission fields of the world.

II. *Our Current Opportunity in the Nation.* For the first time in the history of American Protestantism, one denomination has the numerical strength, the ethnic, social, and racial diversity; and the geographical dispersion to address all of North America with the message of Christ.

III. *Our Crises in Morality, Both Public and Private.* The United States is in a downward spiral of moral decay. Much of the crime and violence is centered in the cities. The ratio of churches to population has declined in all the great cities of America. American Christians no longer have the moral clout they once had. To stem the downward spin toward the dark side of existence we must plan Bible-believing, Bible-living, soul-winning churches in every segment of society.

IV. *Our Concern to be Effective in Evangelism.* The most effective way to reach any people groups for Christ is to plant indigenous churches, faithful to the Father, among that people.

V. *Our Commitment to Obedience.* We want to be obedient to Christ and His Commission. The Spirit-filled church was obedient to the Lord by making disciples and planting churches. So shall we be obedient to Him.

Oh, how desperately we need the mission vision today! In John 4:35 Jesus said, "Say not ye, There are yet four months, and then come the harvest? behold, I say unto you, Lift up your eyes, and look on the fields; for they are white already to harvest." The door of opportunity is open to us now! If we wait too long, the harvest will rot in the field and thousands of unsaved will be lost forever.

May God help us to get the mission vision now before it is too late!

NOTE

1. Peter Wagner, *Church Planting for a Greater Harvest* (Ventura, Calif.: Regal Books, 1990), 19-21.

2

FIELD

"Say not ye, There are yet four months and then cometh harvest? behold, I say unto you, Lift up your eyes, and look on the *fields*" (John 4:35).

The fields Jesus referred to in this familiar passage were not only ripe fields for evangelism but for church planting as well. The apostolic task of the church today is to find that ripe field with the determined intent to evangelize, baptize, congregationalize, and organize a body of Christ in that place.

The local New Testament church is not merely a service club of some sort or another fraternal organization. Nor is it a building made with brick and mortar or steel and stone. The church, in the New Testament sense, is the body of Jesus in that place composed of His disciples gathered for worship and study and then scattered for witness and ministry. The church is to do in that community what Jesus would do if He were there physically.

On one occasion Jesus reminded His disciples that the same works He was doing they would "do also; and greater works than these shall he do" (John 14:12). How can we do greater works than Jesus? He was the greatest preacher that ever preached and the greatest teacher that ever taught. How can any of us do greater works than He?

Jesus was probably not speaking of the quality of work we would perform but rather the quantity of ministry that would be done by the multiplying of His body through local churches. As long as He was on the earth, He was confined to one body in one place at one time. But as His body has been duplicated and replicated throughout the world, through the witness and ministry of Spirit-filled, God-anointed churches, His work has been magnified many times.

Everywhere we plant and grow an evangelistic, ministering church, it is as if we have planted Jesus anew in that place to continue His work even as if He were there physically Himself.

In his book entitled *A Quest for Vitality in Religion*, Finley Edge notes a distinct difference between what he calls "church work" and "the work of the church." He defines church work as the many mundane routines that occupy our time and energy in sustaining the church and maintaining its programs. This would include attending committee meetings, mimeographing the church paper, taking deposits to the bank, preparing the Sunday bulletin, and other tasks. Although all these duties are important, they are not really what the church is all about.

On the other hand Dr. Edge defines the work of the church as being nothing less than to be and do in its community what Jesus would do if He were there physically. This, he concludes, is the real purpose of the church and the justification for its existence.[1]

Further Dr. Edge observes as churches grow in size and years, they tend to be more occupied with church work and less committed to the true work of the church. They tend to become more concerned with maintenance of their programs, organizations, and buildings and less involved in witness, missions, and ministry. What a sad indictment of the churches of our day.

Where then are these many "fields white unto harvest?" How do we find them?

New Suburban Communities

Although in many cities of America the core city—midtown, downtown, and inner city—is in decline, nearly every great metropolitan area has burgeoning suburbs with new subdivisions where hundreds of homes are under construction. The perimeter of many cities is now swarming with new planned communities that are in many ways new cities themselves. There are shopping centers, large supermarkets, and schools. There are service stations and grocery stores, hospitals and Laundromats, parks and parking lots, but where are the churches? In many cases, no land is provided or purchased for any evangelical church of any kind.

The suburban communities of America cry out like the man in the Macedonian vision, "Come over . . . and help us" (Acts 16:9). When community planners are first approached with the prospect of a new subdivision, evangelical Christians should be right on their heels demanding that provision be made for a new church in that community. If resources are not available to buy a tract of land and build a building, efforts should be made to rent or lease temporary space in a school, lodge hall, or some other appropriate, well-located facility. Surely the Lord will place that new community on some church's heart and give the pastor of that church the vision of planting a new congregation in that challenging location.

Evangelical Christians must not allow new communities to spring up across America without determined effort to plant Bible-teaching, soul-winning churches in the midst of that new area.

Downtown and Inner Cities

The greatest fields of opportunity for planting churches in America are often the very areas we have so long neglected and abandoned. When the inner cities found themselves in transition, evangelical churches by the thousands sold their facilities, relocated their congregations, and left the downtown and midtown areas without a witness or ministry.

This is not to fault the church that chooses to relocate. Often this is the wise choice. When most of the congregation has, in fact, relocated to the suburbs, this has, in a sense, relocated the church, even though the building remains downtown. If the church is not willing or able to change its nature to adjust to its changing community, it is probably the wise choice to relocate its building also.

However, if a church elects to relocate to the suburbs, it should follow what is commonly known as the "rule of the forest." If we cut down a tree, we should always plant another in its place. The church that relocates must not in so doing forsake the community it has served. It should make a determined effort to continue a congregation, perhaps a dependent satellite unit, that is homogeneously in sync with the community it is seeking to reach and minister to. That new congregation may meet in the church's former facilities or in a new location. Perhaps multiple congregations could be sponsored in the same facility formerly occupied by the mother church?

The inner cities of America are truly a "field white unto harvest" for church planting, especially predominantly black and ethnic congregations. However, some of the wealthiest and most affluent citizens live in the inner cities as well. Penetrating the high-rise luxury apartment is a formidable challenge to effective church planting!

Most of the ministry centers staffed by the Southern Baptist Convention's Home Mission Board now have what are referred to as "congregational expressions." These are congregations of those reached and ministered to by the ministry center who gather during the week and/or on Sunday morning for Bible teaching, preaching, and worship. Those won to Christ through the redemptive ministries of that center are now nourished, nurtured, and discipled through these indigenous congregations. Likely, most of these people would never attend a typical evangelical church but see the ministry center as their spiritual home not only for their physical but their spiritual needs as well.

A young Baptist preacher had a heavy burden for the runaway teenagers in Toronto, Canada. Many of these teenagers from throughout eastern Canada and the northeastern part of the United States settled on Yong Street in Toronto. They were homeless, jobless, helpless, and hopeless, waiting for someone to care for them and minister to their needs.

The preacher rented a storefront building on Yong Street and began a coffee house ministry. Droves of young people came to this spiritual haven for coffee, a muffin, and a few kind words. The ministry was effective; the witness fruitful; and many of these young people received Jesus as Savior and Lord.

However, congregationalizing these teenagers was another challenge! They were welcome in the typical evangelical churches, even with their long hair, dirty clothes, beads and earrings, but they did not feel comfortable.

"This is our church," they said, "and you are the only pastor we have ever known." So, they formed The Church on Yong Street, a congregation made up of teenagers. They meet every Sunday for worship and several times during the week. The pastor does the preaching and leads the Bible study, but teenagers do all the rest. Teenagers usher, read the Scriptures, share testimonies, sing in the choir, play the instruments, wave the banners; and everyone has a part. The services are power-packed and Spirit-filled! Praise God for The Church on Yong Street, truly an example of "coloring outside the lines."

Multihousing Areas

Already 60 to 65 percent of the people in the major cities of America live in multihousing, that is, apartment buildings, condominiums, town houses, government housing communities, mobile home communities, and the like. It is predicted that by the year 2000, more than 75 percent of the population of the metropolitan areas of the nation will live in this type of housing. However, more than 90 percent of the residents of these multihousing areas are without any local church affiliation of any kind. This is truly a field "white unto harvest."

Again, the First Baptist Church of Arlington, Texas, is the premier example of a church rising to this opportunity to plant churches where the people are. Most of their one hundred plus mission congregations meet in multihousing units, usually in a meeting room or a vacant apartment or some other available space.

In most cases, managers will give permission and many times even donate the meeting space for a new congregation if they can be assured meaningful ministry will be performed, meeting the needs of that housing unit. Day-care services for preschoolers, after-school programs for the children, drug-and-alcohol prevention programs for the youth, chaplaincy services, counseling services for those with marital and family problems are examples of meaningful ministries that can be performed in exchange for making space available for the new mission congregation.

Ethnic and Black Communities

Ours is a rapidly changing, pluralistic society. Vast waves of immigrants are rapidly changing the face of America. Most of the great cities of America no longer have an Anglo majority. Any serious efforts to evangelize and congregationalize the metropolitan areas of this nation must give priority to planting churches among peoples of all ethnic and racial backgrounds.

The Southern Baptist Convention reported over six thousand ethnic congregations and fifteen hundred predominantly black congregations in 1990. The number is growing rapidly. Southern Baptist work among Koreans in the United States began in 1956. By 1990 there were over six hundred Korean Southern Baptist churches in the United States moving rapidly toward the goal of one thousand by 1995. This is only one example of the rapid proliferation of Southern Baptist congregations among those of ethnic background.

The very areas many used to think were unreachable—the transitional communities made up predominantly of ethnics or blacks—are now the most fruitful fields in America for evangelism and church planting. Among Southern Baptists, work in ethnic communities is growing much more rapidly than in Anglo areas. The baptism ratio in ethnic churches is approximately 1 to

12, whereas among Anglo churches it is about 1 to 42. In many cities and several state conventions, our largest and fastest growing churches are ethnic or black congregations. Truly, God is blessing and rewarding our efforts to "disciple all ethnaes."

Institutions

How many of the inmates at the local jail or nearby prison are going to attend your church next Sunday morning? How many at the hospitals or rest homes in your community will be present for your worship service? Many of them can be if you will take the gospel to them instead of hoping somehow they may come to you.

James Greer, pastor of the Donahue Baptist Church near Pineville, Louisiana, got a heavy burden for the inmates at the Louisiana State Penitentiary in Pineville. He discovered there was no evangelical ministry of any kind in that prison. He asked permission to conduct services there every week. As a result, a new church was birthed within the walls of the Louisiana State Penitentiary. Every member is an inmate who has been won to Christ and baptized into the fellowship of this congregation. They now average eighty in attendance and, although only two years old, have already won and baptized forty inmates.

Is this truly a church? After all, there is no building, no steeple or pews, no full-time pastor, and does not meet the traditional concept of what "church" ought to be. However, a good look at the New Testament reveals that "church" in a biblical sense, is not a building with a steeple and pews. In fact, it was probably over one hundred years before any church had its own facility. Rather the church was simply a body of believers gathered for worship, organized for witness and ministry to the community, seeking to be Jesus in the place where they exist. In that sense, the church at Pineville is just as much New Testament, if not more so, than many of the traditional evangelical churches of our day.

Rural Areas

In our burden and concern for the cities, let's not forget the silos! Migrant communities, recreational areas, villages, and small towns where evangelical churches do not exist or are no longer effective are also "fields white unto harvest."

In some areas, especially in the North and West, Southern Baptists are finding the most fruitful results in small rural communities. Strong, Bible-based teaching and preaching coupled with a warm, caring spirit and a friendly atmosphere have met a real need in many of these communities. Many of these new congregations are pastored by bivocationals.

Of course, the rural areas of America have long been populated by small Methodist and Baptist country churches. Many have never had a full-time pastor and have never averaged more than thirty or forty in attendance. But out of these churches have come thousands of pastors, missionaries, evangelists, chaplains, and other Christian servants serving God throughout the world. "Who hath despised the day of small things?" (Zech. 4:10).

In his excellent book on church starting entitled, *Planting New Churches*, Jack Redford suggests several questions that the missions development committee of the local church should ask when considering the beginning of a new work:

> *Does the area have a great unmet need for the witness and ministry of a new church?* Are there a disproportionate number of unchurched people? Are existing churches failing to present an effective gospel witness? Are existing churches failing to minister adequately to the needs of the people in the community?[2]

Certainly all of these are pertinent questions that should be studied carefully and prayerfully as a church considers sponsoring a new work.

Imagine, if you will, a city with a population of 172 million!

Of course, there is no such city in the world today. The largest city in the world is probably Mexico City, Mexico, with approximately thirty million population. Let this city of 172 million represent the number of lost people the Home Mission Board Research Department estimates live in America today. How many new churches do we need to reach this 172 million? Fifteen thousand new churches will not even scratch the need!

The challenge is even greater when you consider that this number of lost people in America is growing by nearly two million every year. The truth is we are losing America much more rapidly than we are winning this nation for Christ.

These 172 million unsaved people represent 172 million reasons we must be earnestly seeking "fields white unto harvest," planting churches wherever the people are.

As you drive through your community, be soul conscious. Ask, "Lord, where is that field white unto harvest? Where do we need to start a new church?" If you ask Him to show you the place, He will do so! Be ready to receive that mission vision from the Lord and plan now to start that new work.

NOTES

1. Finley Edge, *A Quest for Vitality in Religion* (Nashville: Broadman, 1963), 22-32.

2. Jack Redford, *Planting New Churches* (Nashville: Broadman, 1978), 35.

3

FAITHFUL FEW

"The harvest is truly plenteous but the laborers are few. Pray ye therefore the Lord of the harvest that He will send forth laborers into his harvest" (Matt. 9:37-38).

Many look at the fields and conclude the problem is in the harvest. The reason many churches are not growing and new churches are not being planted, they conclude, is that the harvest is lacking. "People are too gospel hardened here," they say. Or, "You can't do it here in this place," for one reason or another.

All of this is foolish, idle chatter that has no foundation in Scripture or experience. The truth is great churches are being established and growing as never before in every part of the nation and the world. Doors of opportunity like never before in history are opening for evangelism and church planting throughout the globe.

The greatest churches in the history of Christendom exist today. Who can visit or hear about the Yoido Full Gospel Church averaging over five hundred thousand in attendance every Sunday and not be utterly amazed!

Likewise, the greatest churches in the history of our nation exist today. Numbers of churches now averaging many thousand in attendance exist in every part of our nation, many of them relatively new congregations.

The Saddleback Valley Community Church in Mission Viejo, California, has had the fastest growth of any Southern Baptist church in history. It was started by Rick Warren and his wife, Kay, in 1980, with just seven people meeting in a living room.

Today this church averages about five thousand in attendance every week and still meets in temporary facilities. (A new worship center and education building are presently under construction.) In fact, since its inception, this burgeoning congregation has met in fifty-three school buildings and has sponsored twenty new missions. What a testimony to what God can do with a "faithful few."

No, the problem is not with the "harvest" but rather with the "laborers." Jesus reminds us that the harvest is plenteous. The problem is that the laborers are so few. Nevertheless, little is much when God is in it! Even a few, just a small handful of people, dedicated to witnessing and ministering in the name of Jesus, can change an entire community.

Someone has said, "The mob is a glob of slob. You can't count on the mob. It is the Master's minority that gets the job done and changes the world."

Certainly, in most cases, it is the "Master's minority" that gets the job done when it comes to planting and growing new churches. Seldom are there great numbers of people waiting in line to help begin a new work.

Ross Hughes, former director of missions for the Capital City Baptist Association in Columbus, Ohio, had a map of Columbus on the wall of his office. A red pin targeted every spot where he envisioned a new work needed to be started. He would often greet one of the pastors of the churches in his association with the question, "Where are you planning to start a new work this year?" If the pastor did not have a ready answer, Ross had one for him. "Would you consider starting a work at so and so?" He was always at the task of enlisting pastors to lead their churches to sponsor a new work in a place of need and opportunity.

Hughes spoke often of the "frontier four." He believed if there were four families who felt led of God to commit themselves to be the nucleus of a new congregation, a church could be started anywhere one was needed. He challenged these four families to "teach, tithe, and tarry."

Assuming the four families consisted of at least six or eight adults, their willingness to "teach" would supply the workers necessary for a fully graded Sunday School. The "tithe" of their incomes would meet or help meet the financial needs of the new mission and, hopefully, would be sufficient, along with the state convention and Home Mission Board assistance, to employ a mission pastor soon. Their willingness to "tarry" meant a commitment to burn the bridges, cut the ties to the mother church, and commit themselves to become a permanent part of this new mission.

It is always wonderful to have good people who will come for a time to assist the new work in getting started. Often they meet a much-needed function, leading the singing, playing the piano, or helping in various other ways. But their commitment is only temporary, and their intention is to soon return to the mother church.

Although these folks are needed and helpful, you cannot build a lasting, stable work on temporary help. There must at least be a nucleus of people willing to make a long-term commitment to making the mission their new church home.

Who are these faithful few that make up the nucleus of the new work and where and how do we find them?

Church Rolls of the Sponsoring Church

Of course, the first place to look will be within the sponsoring church membership itself. The church that is mission-minded and has fulfilling the Great Commission as its primary objective will gladly surrender some members, even leading members, to invest in the beginning of a new work. These people may or may not live in the immediate area of the new congregation, but God has placed a burden on their hearts to birth a new body of Christ in that needy place. They are more than willing, even glad, to leave the luxuries of the mother church, its building and facilities, to meet in a school building, lodge hall, or some other less than commodious facility. They are willing to break the meaningful friendship ties with brothers and sisters they have come to love for the greater cause of establishing a new lighthouse for God in that important place.

The pastor should search church rolls prayerfully and carefully and seek to identify members who could contribute in a meaningful way to a new congregation. He should not hesitate to go to them personally and seek to enlist their support.

Dr. John Bisagno, dynamic pastor of the First Baptist Church of Houston, Texas, declares that he gives a "twofold" invitation every Sunday. "I invite people to come and I invite them to go," he says. Of course, he invites people to join the church and many do. But he also challenges his members to come forward indicating their willingness to leave the mother church and go to one of the twenty-two missions now being sponsored by First Baptist or to help establish another new congregation. With this kind of spirit and mission commitment, God has richly blessed First Baptist Church with a harvest of souls at the mother church and its many missions.

Other Sister Churches

A letter should be sent to every sister church in the area informing the pastor of plans to start a new congregation and identifying the community where it will meet. Pastors should be invited to suggest the names of members in their church who might live in that area or be willing to assist in the beginning of this new work. Soon after the letter has been sent, personal contact should be made with the pastors of sister churches in the area of the new mission. They should be invited to suggest the names of members who might be interested in the new mission.

Unfortunately, some pastors may not be willing to cooperate even though they may have members living in the area where the new work is to begin. They will selfishly want to hold on to their sheep lest someone steal them away. The pastor who thinks this way and his church will be the loser. They will not have the joy of feeling they had some part in the beginning of that new congregation nor will they have the blessing of God that is surely poured out on the mission-minded congregation.

However, there will be pastors and churches who do share the mission vision. They will gladly suggest names and may even contact members who may be interested. They will willingly announce the beginning of the new work from their pulpit and may even put a note in their bulletin or church paper. When the new work is established, they will be able to share in the joy of that victory. God will smile on their sacrificial spirit and bless their church just like He blesses tithers who bring faithfully their tenth to the Lord.

Door-to-Door Survey

A door-to-door survey of the community where the new church is to be birthed is imperative. Mass mailings are good, and telemarketing techniques are effective, but there can be no substitute for a smiling face at the door, meeting the people, leaving information regarding the time and place of the new mission, and getting the names and addresses of any who may be interested.

Of course, there are certain areas where door-to-door survey is difficult, if not impossible. High-rise apartments, restricted condominium areas, and dangerous areas where houses are surrounded by tall fences and locked gates make the task most difficult. In these cases, the survey will have to be by telephone or mail.

However, in most areas, door-to-door visitation is still possible. In this day when many women work outside the home, most canvassing will have to be done in the evenings or on the weekends.

The sponsoring church may wish to have a "survey Sunday," providing lunch for its members and urging them to stay for the meal and two hours of canvassing on Sunday afternoon. While the meal is being eaten, or shortly after, the pastor (or whoever is in charge of the survey effort) can give instructions. A survey sheet or packet of census cards is given to every survey team with a map clearly marking the streets they are to contact. The teams go door-to-door; meeting the people; leaving printed matter about the new mission; and getting the names, addresses, phone numbers, and ages of the children of any who are not regularly attending church. They especially note on the card those who have indicated a positive interest in being a part of the new work. This same type survey can be conducted on a Saturday morning or afternoon or several evenings during a particular week.

Young people make very good canvassers. First Baptist Church of Jacksonville, Florida, has used teams of young people every Saturday surveying the Greater Jacksonville area for many years. A constant number of new prospects are found by these teenage canvassers.

Churches in newer convention territories may want to use summer missionary teams, visiting youth or college choir groups, lay witnessing teams, and other volunteers who are willing to assist in the start of new churches. Again, members of sister churches may also be enlisted to assist in this survey effort.

Telephone Survey and/or Telemarketing

Using the telephone to survey a prospective community where a new church is planned has long been a basic strategy. By purchasing or leasing a "street directory," you can easily identify the family units in the community where the new mission is to exist. Volunteers are enlisted to telephone every family in the area, informing them of the beginning of the new mission, the place where it will be meeting, and inquiring if they would have any interest in attending. Of course, those who indicate interest, and even those who are not interested but do not have a local church home, are recorded on the survey sheets with address, telephone number, and the names and ages of all the children. These then go into the prospect file for evangelistic visitation.

However, in a new and more effective tele-evangelism approach even greater success has been achieved in recent years by using the telephone. In this approach, developed by Norman Wan and outlined in his manual entitled, *Phones for You*, prospects are not only discovered but every effort possible is made to involve them in the beginning of this new work. A series of letters is sent weekly for several months with follow-up telephone calls for several weeks prior to the launch date of the new mission. This approach has proved very successful in most places and is well worth the considerable cost of the manual and the mailouts.

Whether by door-to-door survey or using the telephone, almost invariably some will be found who are more than willing to be part of establishing a new church in their community. It is likely that you will find some who have even been praying that someone would come and start a new Bible-preaching, evangelistic church in their area. Some may even offer the use of their home for fellowship meetings or planning events.

Mass Mailings

If possible, the beginning of a new work should be preceded by a number of mass mailings, blitzing the entire area with an attractive mailout advertising the beginning of this new work. Every area has corporations that specialize in mass mailings. The community can easily be identified by postal zip codes, and bulk mailings to the area at reduced postal rates are a very good investment.

However, it is imperative that the mass mailing be top quality with printed materials (not mimeographed) that are grammatically correct and aesthetically pleasing. A shoddy mailout is worse than useless, signaling the community that the new work will likely be shoddy, also.

If budget allows, a multicolored brochure should be prepared with pertinent information regarding the location of the new work, the times of the services, provision for babies and preschoolers, and other specifics. A map clearly identifying the location of the new mission is most helpful.

The mailout should include a self-addressed, postage-paid reply card, which can be filled out and returned, indicating interest in the new mission and requesting further information. Those who return the card should get a personal visit from someone with a packet of material regarding the new church and urging their commitment to be present for the first Sunday.

Pastor Rick Warren of the Saddleback Valley Community Church in Orange County, California, has used mass mailings as the major tool for advertising their new church throughout Orange County and enlisting prospects for attendance. As a church planter, when the work was first beginning, Warren used his personal savings to fund a major mailout which resulted in over two hundred in attendance on their first Sunday! Saddleback has continued to blitz thousands of homes in Orange County with at least one mass mailout every year. God has blessed and the work has grown phenomenally.

Blitz Day

In addition to the door-to-door survey or mass mailings (or as a poor substitute for these tactics), a community blitz can be helpful. Circulars are printed advertising the beginning of the new church and volunteers from the sponsoring church simply take them door-to-door, leaving them at every home.

Royal Ambassadors, Girls in Action, Acteens, older children's departments or youth groups can effectively conduct a blitz covering thousands of homes on a Saturday morning or afternoon. After the job is complete, you may want to treat the volunteers to a pizza party or hot dog feast, visit a fast-food restaurant, or find some other way to acknowledge their service for the Lord.

One youth group spent a major part of one summer surveying the homes in the Kensington area of Philadelphia, Pennsylvania, preparing to begin a new mission. They borrowed an airport van from a member of the church and dubbed it the "Bapmobile," a takeoff on the Batmobile in Batman and Robin. Every day they loaded in the "Bapmobile" for a trip across the Delaware River into northern Philadelphia, going door-to-door surveying the community. Many prospects were discovered, and by the end of the summer, a new church was established. A bivocational minister, who was a member of the sponsoring church in New Jersey, became the pastor of this new mission. Although it met in a storefront, it became a meaningful lighthouse for God in that north Philadelphia area.

Other Methods

There are at least three additional ways for finding and enlisting the "faithful few" who become the nucleus of the new church.

Pray for Them

Jesus commanded very clearly, "Pray ye therefore the Lord of the harvest that he will send forth laborers" (Matt. 9:38). Just as earnestly as we pray for the lost or we pray for new members or we pray for needed finances, we should pray for the Lord to send forth laborers we need to be part of this new congregation.

You will note that when these disciples began to pray that the Lord would send forth laborers, He sent forth those very disciples themselves (Matt. 10:5). When you pray for laborers, expect that God may answer by sending *you*, or at least sending some of your own fine members. Nevertheless rejoice, for there can be no greater investment on the part of any person or church than starting a new church where one is needed.

Preach for Them

Another means of finding the workers needed is to preach for them. Jesus was constantly preaching for laborers, challenging

His followers to be fervent witnesses faithfully doing the work of the Lord. Every pastor should be mission minded with the world on his heart and a challenge to service on his lips.

The prophet of God who is unwilling to call his people to missionary commitment and to give them up to missions service, should be ashamed! Everyone must some day stand before the judgment seat of Christ to give account to God. Woe to that pastor who has not been faithful in proclaiming the challenge of Christian service, not only in his own church but wherever God leads. God will surely bless the pastor who leads his church to faithful, generous, even sacrificial mission commitment.

Personally Enlist Them

Jesus also taught the importance of personally enlisting the laborers we need to evangelize and plant churches.

Do you remember the parable of the husbandman in Matthew 20? This farmer needed some laborers to work in his vineyard. He went out early in the morning to hire laborers to work in his vineyard. Even though they responded positively, there was still much work to be done. So he went out the third hour of the day and again, finding some idle, he said, "Come work in my vineyard." He repeated this the sixth hour, the ninth hour, and even until the eleventh hour of the day. All day long he was busy at the task of personally enlisting laborers so the harvest would not perish.

It's interesting to note their response to the question, "Why stand ye . . . idle?" Their response may well be the reason many church members are not involved in mission service today. "Because no man hath hired us," they replied. In other words, no one had asked them to serve. No one had challenged them with the need. No one had explained to them the opportunity which was theirs if they would labor faithfully and receive just reward for their labor. When the husbandman went to them personally and explained the challenge, many were willing and ready to serve. (See vv. 1-7.)

There can be no substitute for personal contact. Those starting a new mission should not only discover and identify those who may be interested, but should make every effort possible to enlist them personally, urge their participation, challenge them with the opportunity, assign them a specific task, explain to them the need of a new church in that community, and urge their commitment to be part of the new work.

Ray Cockerell of Fort Worth, Texas, had happily served for years as a deacon in the Polytechnic Baptist Church. His wife, Blanche, was a faithful worker also, serving as the church dietitian. One day, Ray received the distressing news that he was being transferred in his government job to Absecon, New Jersey. What a heartbreak for a man who had lived all his life in Texas, loved his church, and had no desire to leave the South. To be transferred to an unknown town in a Northeastern city was almost more than he could bear. He was distressed and disheartened beyond words.

His college student son had been reading a book by T. B. Maston entitled *God's Will and Your Life*. The book was lying on the coffee table in the living room. One day Ray picked up the book, thumbed through its pages, and his eyes fell on these words,

> Still another decision is 'where one works.' God may want you as a business or professional person or as a government employee to go to some needy area in the homeland or work in a foreign country. Thus you could just as truly become an ambassador for Christ as the so-called missionary.[1]

Of course, Ray and Blanche saw this as an obvious answer to prayer. With new joy in their hearts, they moved to New Jersey only to discover that a new church had recently been started in that small town, meeting in a community hall. Immediately, Ray and Blanche became leaders in that new congregation as it grew from a small mission to a thriving church with a lovely new building. Throughout the years, Absecon Baptist Church has started several Southern Baptist congregations in the South Jersey area.

God raises up His workers when they are needed in the very places they are needed.

When Tillie Burgin, minister of missions at the First Baptist Church of Arlington, Texas, was asked where they found the pastors to lead all these new missions their church was starting, her answer was somewhat surprising. One might think that because Arlington is located so close to Southwestern Baptist Theological Seminary, the largest seminary in the world, that many of these pastors would be ministerial students from that great school. Also, in the area nearby is a Baptist college with many ministerial students who might be effective student church planters in the Arlington area. Indeed a few of the leaders for these new missions are ministerial students. But most were not very interested when they discovered these mission pastors received no salary. Their work is a work of grace just like those who function in other responsibilities in the church.

"The Lord just raises them up," Tillie said with her arms outstretched toward heaven. Very simply, she meant that from within the congregation of the First Baptist Church itself the Lord had anointed and appointed certain people, laymen and laywomen, to lead in the establishment of these new works.

Yes, the Lord works that way, doesn't He? He just "raises them up" at the very time they are needed and for the very place it is His will for a new work to begin.

NOTE

1. T. B. Maston, *God's Will and Your Life* (Nashville: Broadman Press, 1964).

4

FACILITIES

"Greet Priscilla and Aquila my helpers in Christ Jesus. Likewise greet the church that is in their house" (Rom. 16:3,5).

The *oikos* (house church) was not an exception in the New Testament day. Rather, apparently most of the early apostolic churches met in the homes of various members for Bible study, worship, communion, prayer, and praise. Most historians agree that it was at least one hundred years after Christ before any New Testament church had its own facility.

True, many early Christians met regularly in the synagogues and temple for worship with their Jewish brethren. But as the Christian community became a distinct entity within itself, separate from the Jewish tradition, the "house church" became their haven as well as their place of worship.

The "house church" continues today as a mainstay of Christendom. Most new churches begin in somebody's home for fellowship, Bible study, planning, and prayer; but as the group grows, generally they move to a larger facility and eventually to their own property and building. However, in many places in America, and around the world the house church continues as the norm rather than the exception.

Even in the midst of severe persecution, when apparently all semblance of Christianity had been destroyed, we are now amazed to discover that the cause of Christ thrived and grew in Communist China. Continuing their ministry behind closed doors and drawn window shades, small groups of believers gathered in somebody's home. Despite every effort of an atheistic government to rid their land of Christians and the Christian faith, today some estimate as many as fifty million believers live in Communist China, worshiping in more than twenty thousand house churches, as well as in over five thousand church buildings again open for worship.[1]

The idea that the church is a building or must have its own building to function adequately is a myth, certainly contrary to every example we have in the Scriptures.

As previously mentioned, the Saddleback Valley Community Church in Mission Viejo, California, has had the fastest growth of any Southern Baptist church in history yet has never had its own building. This church has grown from a small group of seven people to an average attendance of five thousand, meeting in elementary and high school buildings throughout Orange County.

It is Rick Warren's deep conviction that most churches buy land and build a building before they have sufficient resources to purchase an ideal site and build an attractive, commodious facility. As a result, he believes the small building, poorly located, squelches the future development of the church. "We shape the building and the building then shapes us," is one of his favorite sayings. Warren believes a church would be wise to meet in temporary facilities for several years, at least until it grows enough to purchase the very best possible site and build an attractive facility that will be a help rather than a hindrance in the further growth of the congregation.

Common Myths About Facilities

There are a number of myths that need to be dispelled as we set about to plant new churches.

The New Building Syndrome

One prominent myth is the idea that we simply must have a new building before we will be able to impact or reach the community effectively. This myth is especially prevalent when churches or denominations are seeking to establish new work in affluent suburban areas.

"No matter how hard you try, 'yuppies' and 'baby boomers' who drive big cars and live in fancy homes will not worship in somebody's school building or lodge hall," one church planter declared emphatically.

Saddleback is certainly not the only church that gives the lie to that kind of thinking. New churches throughout America, north, south, east, and west, are being started in affluent, suburban communities meeting in temporary facilities, growing rapidly, and thriving on every hand. At the same time, other churches in beautiful facilities already established are plateaued or declining.

Although the building can and should be an important tool in reaching people and a testimony to the community where it is located, buildings do not reach people. People reach people. If the church, regardless of where it meets, is a warm, loving, caring fellowship with a strong emphasis on evangelistic outreach, it will likely grow no matter where it may meet for worship.

Some new churches are fortunate enough to have as their sponsor a strong, wealthy church which assumes responsibility for purchasing the land and building a building even before the new mission is begun. From the very beginning, the new congregation meets in a building already provided at a location already determined.

There is much to be said for this approach. The new congregation is spared the frustration of meeting in inadequate, temporary facilities, searching for property, arranging loans, and making sacrificial financial gifts to buy land and build a building. The congregation doesn't even help in the erection of the new facility, painting walls, laying floor tile, and landscaping the grounds. How wonderful! It's all been provided with no sweat, toil, or sacrifice on the part of the new congregation.

Suppose a father says to his daughter and new son-in-law, "Honey, I have great news for you! As a wedding gift, I am giving you and your new husband a house. I've already bought it and paid for it and it's yours, free for nothing!"

I am sure this daughter and son-in-law would be grateful. But it would never really be their house. In their minds at least, it would always be "Daddy's house." They had no part in determining where it would be located. They had no say in its design, and they made no sacrifice for its acquisition.

Probably, in the long run, Daddy would be wise to let the young couple struggle awhile, live in a rented apartment, dream, and save toward the day when they could purchase their own home, then at last move in with the joy of knowing it is truly theirs. "We worked for it and saved for it and it is our own."

A group of laymen from a large church in Texas lamented that they did not have the resources to begin new congregations, even though there were scores of places in their city where new work needed to be started.

"Several years ago," they explained, "we spent over a million dollars purchasing land for a new church in a rapidly growing Dallas suburb. However, when the new mission got started, it decided it did not want the location we had purchased for them and refused to assume the indebtedness. They have since constituted as a church, purchased a more desirable site, and have built a new facility. We are left stuck with the land and a debt of over a million dollars, and we can't sell it for even half that amount."

Of course, there are times when new planned communities are developing and if land is not purchased or at least under option soon, an ideal location may be lost. If there is a church, association, state convention, or denominational entity that can purchase this land when "opportunity knocks," it may be a good thing. However, for the most part, it is probably better for the new congregation to have a say in site selection as well as the construction of the first facility.

The Nice-Building Syndrome

Closely akin to the new-building syndrome is the nice-building syndrome. Again, the myth is that, especially in affluent suburban communities of high-income families, people simply cannot be reached unless an attractive, commodious, building is erected from the outset. Certainly, in that type area, when the first unit is constructed it must be first class. Shoddy, second-rate, unattractive, and poorly designed facilities will not make it in the affluent suburbs.

The building becomes a testimony to the community of the dedication and commitment of those who worship there. A shoddy building is evidence of a shoddy dedication on the part of the members. This is unacceptable to the young adults of our day.

However, the idea that even in an affluent community a church has to begin in a nice, well-appointed facility is a myth.

My wife and I are members of a new congregation in an affluent Atlanta suburb. Many members of the church live in large, expensive homes; and the parking lot has its fair portion of Cadillacs, Continentals, Mercedes, and BMWs. However, this new congregation began in the gymnasium of a local elementary school. This multipurpose facility was a metal building with very few windows and no air conditioning. A large exhaust fan roared overhead while we attempted to worship sitting on metal folding chairs gathered in the middle of the gym. During the summer months temperatures rose to over one hundred degrees. No one wore a coat or a tie, not even the pastor. On Sunday evenings we met in the homes of various members.

The church grew and prospered even while meeting in such undesirable facilities. New members were added nearly every Sunday. The fellowship was sweet as members prayed together and planned for the future.

The church now has a lovely, new facility that is spacious and well-located. The members themselves, along with six different teams of missionary builders, constructed the new facility. They had part in its design and construction.

The Big-Building Syndrome

Many churches make a tragic decision to build a facility much larger than is needed. They reason that as soon as the building is constructed, scores of people will attend who had not previously been reached. They mistakenly believe that the building itself will attract great numbers when often that is not the case. Also, they think a large building will be more impressive and make a greater impact on their community.

So, they spend much more than they need to spend building a building far bigger than they need, strapping the church with an exorbitant debt burden, and radically increasing the cost of maintenance and utilities.

Most tragic of all, nothing is more depressing than an unfilled sanctuary. A small number in a large auditorium creates a psychology of defeat. That same number worshiping in a smaller facility will appear victorious, and a success attitude will develop. It is much better to build a smaller first unit with a master plan for orderly expansion.

Providing Facilities

What are some of the options the Missions Development Council of the church should explore as they consider beginning a new work? Where can this new work meet temporarily or even permanently?

A Member's Home

Many, if not most, new churches begin in somebody's home. At least the initial fellowship meetings, usually meeting from three to six months on a weekday evening, are in some member's home or several members' homes. However, some continue meeting in homes permanently, as has been the case in Communist China and other areas.

The "cell church" idea has spread like wildfire. The prime example is probably the Yoido Full Gospel Church in Seoul, Korea, now averaging over five hundred thousand in weekly attendance in seven worship services every Sunday. However, the real key to the growth of the Yoido Church has been over six thousand cell groups meeting throughout Seoul in members' homes every week. Some meet in the evenings, but most meet during the day. Every one of these cell groups has a "shepherd" who pastors that small house church congregation. They meet for prayer, praise, Bible study, and worship. The shepherd, led by the Holy Spirit, determines the agenda. Members of the cell group seek to enlist their neighbors, friends, and relatives to attend the weekly meetings of the house church. Once involved in the house church, they are then encouraged to meet for celebration with the larger congregation at the Yoido central church on Sundays. These cell groups serve as feeders, enlisting people throughout Seoul for weekly Sunday attendance at the mother church.

When a cell group grows to fifteen members it divides, creating two cells for every one. Through this means of geometric progression, in a few short years Pastor Paul Cho has led his church to saturate Seoul with viable, vibrant, witnessing, ministering house churches in nearly every neighborhood of that huge city of eleven million.

However, there is a dimension of the phenomenal success of the Yoido church that must not be neglected. Over thirty thousand members gather every Friday evening for an all-night prayer meeting! Literally thousands gather every morning at 5:00 a.m. for prayer and stay on their knees before God until it's time to leave for work.

Any attempt to explain the phenomenal growth of the Yoido Full Gospel Church or many of the other rapidly growing churches of Korea must not ignore this spiritual dimension. Not only the largest Assembly of God Church, Yoido Full Gospel, but also the largest Presbyterian Church, the largest Methodist Church, and perhaps the largest Baptist Church in the world are all in Seoul, Korea. Thousands of others throughout Korea are growing phenomenally. But in every case, Friday evening, all-night prayer meetings and early morning 5:00 a.m. prayer services are the norm, not the exception. One wonders what would be the results in America, with or without cell groups, if large numbers of our congregation met every morning at 5:00 a.m. for an hour or more of prayer and stayed up every Friday night all night long in prayer meetings at the church.

"If my people, which are called by my name, shall humble themselves, and pray, and seek my face, and turn from their wicked ways, then will I hear from heaven, and will forgive their sin, and will heal their land" (2 Chron. 7:14).

The cell group concept is being used effectively in America in many places. Often the pattern is similar to that in Korea, with congregations meeting for Bible study and worship on Sunday mornings. But rather than the typical Sunday evening worship service, members assemble in cell groups or house churches throughout their city, seeking to enlist neighbors, friends, and relatives who might come to their homes for Bible study and worship, but likely would not travel to the mother church.

A House

For either a temporary or permanent facility, a vacant house purchased, leased, or rented can often be remodeled and adapted as an adequate church facility. In Puerto Rico, most Southern Baptist churches meet in facilities that were formerly houses for typical families of four or five people. In most cases, what was the living room becomes a small sanctuary or sometimes the living room and dining area combine to form the chapel area. Bedrooms become Sunday School rooms and even the basement and/or attic may be utilized.

The Delaware Valley Baptist Church in Willingboro, New Jersey, met in a house for about ten years. The basement was converted into a small sanctuary seating eighty people. The rest of the building housed Sunday School rooms. A former chicken house and a two-car garage were remodeled, providing additional Sunday School space. However, even that was not adequate, so several former school buses were purchased to be used for a bus ministry but also to house Sunday School departments and classes. In addition, the pastor's home was used for a college and career department with classes meeting in the bedrooms. Finally, additional space was provided by renting two elementary schools nearby and shuttling students to and from the church building, using church buses. Three worship services in the small house church auditorium accommodated attendance exceeding three hundred, while children's worship was conducted in one of the school buildings and youth worship in another. The Lord blessed; the church grew rapidly and was one of the leading churches in its state convention in baptisms.

School Buildings

In most cases, the most appropriate facility for beginning a new work, if available, is a local school. Unfortunately, many communities no longer allow new congregations to rent a school building, believing this is somehow a violation of church/state separation. However, in many places they are still available and are a godsend.

School buildings are usually well-located, attractive, and commodious. If classrooms are available, they will be equipped with age-graded furniture, making it suitable for graded Sunday School classes.

When renting a school, it is imperative to maintain good relationships with the local school principal and the custodians. It is a good idea to do something extra for these people from time to time. Perhaps the pastor and his wife could take the principal and his/her spouse to dinner or invite them for an evening in their home. At the least, drop by the school frequently to visit with the principal and be sure there are no problems to be resolved. A generous gratuity for the custodian from time to time will do much to create good relations.

Keep in mind, if either the principal, custodian, or a number of the teachers become upset at the church, you will likely lose the use of this facility. Do whatever you can to create and continue good relationships with the personnel at the school.

Parsons Baptist Church in Columbus, Ohio, met in the Parsons Elementary School for more than three years, growing from sixteen members to over three hundred in attendance before they finally built a new building. On several occasions they had over four hundred for worship while meeting in this lovely school building.

Probably the most popular place to begin a new work, especially in suburban communities, is in a school facility. However, this is generally only a temporary arrangement for the new church that expects within a reasonable period of time to have its own property and building.

Lodge or Community Halls

Nearly any community will have a number of lodge halls, community rooms in banks, shopping malls, fire halls, etc. Ask around and make a list of available facilities. In most cases, these facilities can be made available to a church for a minimal fee.

Game Rooms and Community Rooms in Apartment Buildings

Most large apartment communities, whether low-income government apartments, affluent high-rises, condominiums, or retirement centers, will have some kind of assembly area. It may be a community room, game room, or dining area. With the proper approach to the manager or owner, these areas will be made available to a new church for worship and Bible study. The likelihood of acquiring the use of these areas is greatly enhanced if a meaningful weekday ministry is also provided, meeting the needs of those who live in the apartments. Providing a twenty-four-hour-a-day, on-call chaplaincy service or day-care service for preschoolers are attractive possibilities. Weekday programs for children and youth, counseling services, drug or alcohol rehabilitation programs, Bible schools, and backyard Bible clubs are other possibilities that will be very attractive to the managers of apartment units.

Many times the management will allow the new congregation to use a vacant apartment. This has proved very successful many times in many places. You may offer the owner a "charitable gift in kind" in exchange for the free use of a community room or apartment. The sponsoring church simply sends a letter to the owner certifying that he has contributed an amount equal to the fair rental value of the apartment or game room which he can use for income tax purposes.

A layman from the Parsons Baptist Church in Columbus, Ohio, had a heavy burden for the Lincoln Park government housing project. Here were the lower-income people, many on welfare, elderly on small pensions, and unmarried mothers living on AFDC. Most had no local church affiliation and rarely attended a local congregation. This layman, who was also an ordained Baptist minister and insurance salesman, asked permission to hold services in the community room of the project. The Parsons Baptist Church agreed to sponsor him and this new work, calling it the Lincoln Park Baptist Mission. After knocking on every door and meeting all the residents, informing them of the new congregation, they met for their first Sunday with over forty in attendance. Soon attendance had climbed to fifty, with many residents of the housing project coming to know Jesus Christ as Savior and Lord and becoming active members of the new congregation. The work continued as a viable witness in that project, ministering to many needs and reaching people for Christ nearly every week.

However, after several years the pastor and congregation decided they needed their own building. Like many new congregations, they became obsessed with the "we've got to have our own church" syndrome. They discovered an old, large house just a few blocks from the project for a reasonable price. So they purchased the old house, remodeled it, and relocated the congregation from the community center in the housing project to this new building just a few blocks away. Sadly, within a short time the congregation dwindled to very few and finally disbanded. Once they had moved from the housing project into the surrounding community, they were on a different turf. The community and the project simply did not mix. People from the community would not venture into the project, especially for worship. Likewise, people from the project did not feel ownership, relationship, or fellowship with the surrounding neighborhood. It would probably have been much wiser to have continued meeting in the community room indefinitely. The community room was the nerve center for the entire project. Residents came there daily to play bingo and checkers, read magazines, play games, and to receive their mail. The community room was theirs. Likewise, the congregation meeting there on Sunday was theirs. They felt true and genuine ownership, even though the facility was rented. Once they relocated, they no longer felt that ownership, even though they technically owned the building.

Motel or Hotel Conference Rooms

The great cities of America are saturated with hotels and motels both in suburban areas and downtown. Many new churches are using conference rooms as the meeting place for both Sunday School and worship.

Often, especially in the large cities, this may be the only option. The rental cost is sometimes exorbitant but often, with the proper approach and a sympathetic management, motel and hotel conference rooms can be rented for a minimal fee. Again, it is appropriate to suggest a charitable gift in kind in exchange for free or partial payment for the rent of the facilities. Also, think of ways the new congregation can be of service to the motel. Are you willing to provide twenty-four-hour-a-day, on-call chaplaincy services for the hotel guests and staff? Are you willing to provide free counseling services for the hotel staff and/or guests? Wouldn't worship services every Sunday morning for all the guests be attractive to most managers? You might even agree to provide a printed invitation to the guests to attend the worship services which could be placed under the doors or in the mail slots every Saturday evening.

Another Church Building or the Sponsoring Church's Building

If the new church is being started in the same geographical area of the sponsoring church, why not share the same facility? Perhaps the sponsoring church is an Anglo church in a transitional community and has seen the vision of starting an ethnic or black congregation or a church targeting a different socioeconomic group in the same area. Using the building for multiple congregations is a tremendous idea, especially in transitional communities.

First Baptist Church, Westminster, California, was, at one time, a strong Anglo congregation averaging about four hundred in attendance. However, as is often the case, the community changed radically with many Anglos fleeing to other areas while a diversity of ethnic groups moved in. The Anglo congregation declined to about 150 people.

However, several years ago First Baptist Church got the vision of growing by extension rather than expansion. Today, six congregations meet in the church's facility, now called the Golden West Worship Center. In addition to the Anglo congregation, there is a Vietnamese, a Japanese, a Korean, a Hispanic, a deaf, and a Messianic Jewish Fellowship all sharing the same facilities. Total attendance is now over eight hundred, nearly twice as many as they ever averaged as a single congregation.[2]

Also, the use of sister church buildings of your same denomination or even some other denomination are potential locations for a new work. Many new Southern Baptist congregations meet in Seventh-Day Adventist buildings and even in Jewish synagogues. Often, especially in transitional communities, declining Anglo congregations, regardless of the denomination, are more than happy to share their facilities with a new ethnic or black congregation, regardless of its denominational affiliation.

The Brazilian Baptist Church, a new congregation in Philadelphia, Pennsylvania, meets in a beautiful Methodist Church which had dwindled to about twenty in attendance. They have full use of this facility for a rental cost sufficient to cover the cost of utilities. The generous spirit of this fine Methodist congregation has enabled Baptists to establish a strong ethnic congregation averaging over sixty in attendance.

This story could be duplicated many times with many examples throughout the nation. Many ethnic congregations are willing and even prefer to meet on Sunday afternoons rather than Sunday morning, making it feasible for two or three congregations to share the same building without disrupting in any way the services and programs of other congregations.

The Southcliff Baptist Church in Fort Worth, Texas, began as a mission meeting on Sunday afternoons in a Congregational Church building. It soon moved to the Westcliff Elementary School where it met until property was purchased and a first-unit building was erected at its present location.

My wife and I were members of the East Shore Baptist Church in Harrisburg, Pennsylvania, while I served on the state staff of the Baptist Convention of Pennsylvania-South Jersey. This congregation met weekly in a beautiful Seventh-Day Adventist building and continued in that lovely facility for several years.

The shared use of church buildings has long been a well-proven means of establishing new churches.

Unique Alternatives

The sky is the limit when it comes to finding facilities to begin a new work. People with a vision from God and a heavy burden to establish a new body of Christ in a place where it is needed will always find a place for that new congregation to meet.

Ken Evans had a heavy burden for a Bohemian section of Atlanta called Little Five Points. Here teenagers and young adults roam the streets, visit the several New Age book stores, browse through the Mideastern boutiques, eat in the Indian and Eastern-style restaurants, and mainly lounge in a nearby park playing guitars, singing ballads, and dialoguing.

Even though local churches of all denominations surround the area, none were reaching these young people for Christ. Ken realized if they were to be reached, the church would have to go to them. So he began conducting services in the park every Sunday morning. Contemporary-style music with guitars and bongo drums gathers the crowd. They joyfully enter into the singing, even though the songs were Christian choruses with a salvation message. At the appropriate moment, Evans shares a simple gospel message, direct and to the point, and gives an invitation. They are known as the In-town Fellowship sponsored by the Christ Community Baptist Church of Atlanta.

Fred Kerr is a Baptist preacher from Columbia, South Carolina. In the summer of 1988 he came to Atlanta to participate in "Operation Rescue," a group dedicated to opposing abortion by marching in front of abortion clinics, joining hands and arms to prohibit those who would enter the clinic from doing so. As a result, Fred and many others were arrested for trespassing, brought before a local judge, and sentenced to jail. In exchange for his effort to prohibit the murder of unborn babies, Fred received a ninety-day sentence in the Fulton County jail in Atlanta.

As any good Baptist preacher should, while in jail he began to witness to the inmates. He found many receptive to his gospel witness and many inmates prayed to receive Jesus. He began to meet with these new believers (and others who would attend), for Bible study every morning and evening. Others were saved and the group began to grow in number as well as spirit.

It occurred to Fred that when his ninety-day term would end, the group would likely disband, the Bible studies and worship discontinue, and much of what was gained would be lost unless something could be done to create a continuing structure. So, he led the group to organize as the "Church at Bellwood" (the name of the prison unit where Fred and the others were incarcerated). From the group itself, he trained Bible study leaders, worship leaders, and one particular man that he perceived God had called to be the leader of the group. When Fred's jail term ended, he returned to Columbia, South Carolina, but the Church at Bellwood continued. This is just another example of a new congregation being birthed in a place where its witness and ministry was desperately needed, even though in a most unlikely place according to any traditional standard. You can read the story of the Church at Bellwood in Fred Kerr's book entitled *Ninety Days for Life*.

Surely there is no end of opportunity in finding a location to gather believers and form a congregation in the place where that witness and ministry is needed.

Its Own Building

Historically, most new churches dream of and plan for their own property and building. Just like most newly married couples dream of a day when they will own their own home, most new congregations wish for their own church home with building and facilities they can call their own and do with as they wish.

However, especially in metropolitan areas, the cost of land is so prohibitive and construction costs so exorbitant that it may not be feasible for many new churches in those areas to own their own land and building. Like thousands of businesses and corporations, they may have to exist forever in rented or leased facilities.

Many churches are caught up in a "field of dreams" mentality—"If you build it, they will come!" Empty church buildings throughout the land attest that buildings alone will not reach people. People, not buildings, reach people.

Perhaps one reason for the phenomenal success of certain campus ministries such as Campus Crusade and Inter-Varsity Christian Fellowship is that they have never owned their buildings and, therefore, have not had to pay off large indebtedness on loans. They could concentrate their energies and finances in the most important task of reaching people for Christ and ministering to their needs. Also, because they did not own their facilities, they located their work right in the middle of those they were seeking to reach, namely the student center, which, almost invariably, is the hub of activity for the campus. Had they owned their own building, likely it would have been located several blocks from the mainstream, housed in a facility far removed from the students they were seeking to reach.

Nevertheless, a beautiful, attractive, well-located church building can be a tremendous tool for the establishment of a permanent, functioning body of Christ, especially in a suburban or rural community. Owning its own building allows the church to offer a full program of activities, not only Sunday Bible study, training, and worship, but weekday activities as well. The church becomes a precious, spiritual home for its congregation. As a family, they worship there regularly, their children are married there, and the funerals of family members may be conducted in the sanctuary. The church becomes a hallowed place in the minds and thoughts of the members. No wonder we have often thought of the church and the church building as inseparable.

Location.—When purchasing a home, clients are often reminded by real estate agents that the three most important considerations are (1) location, (2) location, and (3) location. If true at all, this is even more so when considering the purchase of land for a new church building.

George Fletcher says, "Anytime you see a sign saying 'such and such a church, one half mile,' they should have put the church where the sign is." There is more truth to that than fiction.

Often the most expensive property a church will ever own is a piece somebody gives them. Never skimp when you consider the purchase of land for a church site. Purchasing a site off the main traffic flow will almost invariably confine the church's ministry and outreach to a neighborhood rather than the larger community.

It is important that the church site be on a main traffic artery, easily accessible to the largest area possible and highly visible to all the citizens of that area. Ideally the church should be located in such a place that every member of the community will have occasion to see it every day.

Another important consideration is topography. If possible, the land on which the church will be built should be high and dry. Purchasing land that requires extensive grading and development will mean vast amount of resources deflected from construction for land preparation. Sometimes even extensive preparation will not overcome the problems inherent in bad terrain.

Again, it is imperative that proper testing be done to assure the site is acceptable. Is there a toxic waste problem? Is there rock or stone underground that will cause great difficulty in construction? Has all or a portion of the land been declared as floodplain or wetlands? Only a qualified, certified architect or land engineer can adequately answer these questions. It will cost something to get the information you need, but you dare not purchase land without it.

Of course, zoning has to be an important consideration. Is the property zoned for a church or will you have to get a variance? This too must be checked with your local zoning board, and any sales agreement should always have a contingency to provide an escape in case the needed zoning variances and permits are not forthcoming. You need a lawyer to help you prepare the sales agreement to assure the contract is buyer friendly. In most cases you need to purchase a minimum of three acres if you expect to ever grow beyond 400 in attendance. A good "rule of thumb" is one acre for every 150 you anticipate in attendance. In fact, in most municipal areas, you will have to have at least one parking space for every three seats provided in your sanctuary or you will not be able to get a permit for construction. Regardless of what attendance may be, building permits are based on the maximum number provided for in the facility.

Cost is also an important factor. Any amount you borrow for land or construction has to be paid back, and generally a congregation is very unwise to assume indebtedness that takes more than one third of its income to amortize. Another good "rule of thumb" is that one week's offering should be sufficient to make the monthly debt payment. Anything beyond this amount, and certainly beyond 30 percent, will likely be draining funds desperately needed for staff salaries, program costs, maintenance of the building and facilities, advertising, promotion, and world missions. The end result of an exorbitant debt load is a demoralized congregation that has lost its enthusiasm and its ability to reach and minister to its community effectively. A building isn't that important. Keep the debt load as low as possible.

When an appropriate site has been located, and the congregation is ready to purchase, most denominations have some type of grant or loan provision for site purchase. For many years the Home Mission Board of the Southern Baptist Convention has maintained a Division of Church Loans with a total portfolio now exceeding one hundred million dollars, either already lent or available mostly to new churches ready to purchase a site and/or build their first unit. At the present the Church Loans Division is able to service all qualified applicants. Basically, a qualified applicant is a new congregation affiliated with the Southern Baptist Convention and able to amortize their loan with not more than 30 percent of their present income.

Planning.—Once a site has been purchased, the new congregation is ready to make plans toward building its first unit. (It is usually unwise to make extensive building plans before a site is purchased. The shape and nature of the building is often determined by the geography and topography of the site itself.)

The first step is for the pastor to appoint (or the committee on committees to select) a building steering committee. This committee does not need to be composed of people who have building design or construction expertise. Rather this is a committee representing a broad section of the congregation, especially those who lead the various programs. This committee will lead in the search for an architect and will make a recommendation to the church. They will then work with the architect in developing a floor plan and the basic design of the new building. After the pastor and committee have agreed on the architectural design, a recommendation will be made to the church for their approval.

At this time, a construction committee will be formed. The

construction committee will be composed of members who have expertise in construction and detailed building design, plus some representatives from the steering committee. They will work closely with the architect in submitting the plans for a bid to a contractor, receiving the bids, determining the best contractor for the job, and then presenting a recommendation to the church. They will then work carefully with the architect, assisting in acquiring the necessary permits and in supervising the construction of the new building.

However, before the building plans are completed, it is imperative that the plans be submitted to your denomination's architectural services. Southern Baptists should send their plans to the Church Architecture Department, Baptist Sunday School Board, 127 Ninth Avenue, North, Nashville, Tennessee 37234. They will review the plans to assure they are designed adequately to accommodate a Southern Baptist congregation with its various programs, make suggestions as to how the plans could be improved, and provide much needed information. If a loan is being pursued through the Home Mission Board, it is required that the plans be approved by the Church Architecture Department before the loan is consummated.

Many architects simply do not understand the many-faceted programs of a Southern Baptist church, including Sunday School, Discipleship Training, missions organizations, etc. They often tend to be "sanctuary minded," anxious to build a beautiful worship center that will be a testimony to their own artistry but often totally ignoring the important educational and training function of the church.

New congregations affiliated with the Southern Baptist Convention are wise to order from the Church Architecture Department the several booklets of suggested floor plans for new units and prayerfully consider which one of these, if any, would meet the needs of the congregation. This should be done at the outset of the planning process, even before an architect has been employed. A consultant from the Baptist Sunday School Board will gladly arrange to meet with the pastor and the steering committee to discuss planning for the new building. At no charge to the congregation, they will design an appropriate space plan schematic based on pertinent data from your own particular congregation. This space plan recommendation can be shared with the architect as a guide for the development of the architectural renderings. However, the Church Architecture Department cannot serve as an architect for the church. Most state laws require that a local architect be contracted.[3] (See appendix, pp. 169-71.)

In recent years, literally thousands of missionary builders have assisted new churches in constructing their first unit, often reducing the cost of construction by 50 percent or more. New Southern Baptist congregations can arrange for this kind of assistance by contacting the Volunteer Division of the Home Mission Board, 1350 Spring Street, NW, Atlanta, Georgia 30367. In 1991 more than four hundred groups, totaling more than eight thousand volunteer builders built over one hundred churches for Southern Baptists throughout the United States.

When using volunteer builders, it is important to coordinate every effort with the project coordinator. He will assist in the purchase of materials so they are ready and on the premises when the first volunteer builder team arrives. If a new congregation is building a small first-unit building, it is not unusual for the team to have the building under roof and 75 percent complete at the end of the first week. Sometimes they even have a worship service in the new building on the Sunday following the team's arrival when the week before there was nothing on the premises but a stack of materials. What a thrill and joy that can be! (However, it is usually not wise to occupy the new building permanently until construction is totally or almost totally completed.)

Yes, a new congregation must have a place to meet. That place may be a beautiful new building, well-located in a growing community or it may be a building the church has purchased from another congregation, which has been remodeled and refurbished appropriately. Or it may be a lodge hall, a community room, or even an open park. It may be in some member's home or a house that has been rented or purchased.

But if a body of believers is gathering there regularly for Bible study, worship, and the preaching of God's Word, it is "church!" In that place, wherever it is, they become the body of Jesus carrying on His work. They are the incarnation of the gospel in that place pointing people to a loving, saving God and ministering in His name.

It was said of the early New Testament church, "Ye have filled Jerusalem with your doctrine" (Acts 5:28), and "These that have turned the world upside down" (17:6) for Jesus. And all this without a building!

Literally thousands of new churches need to be started throughout America with the full understanding that many of them may never have their own property and building. If there are people in that place, there needs to be a vital, viable, witnessing, loving, caring, ministering church in the midst of them regardless of where they meet.

NOTES

1. Lewis Myers, Regional Vice President, Cooperative Services International, Foreign Mission Board (conversation).

2. Bruce Stokes, pastor of First Baptist Church, Westminister, California (conversation January 16, 1992)

3. Steve Newton, architect, Church Architecture Department, Sunday School Board (conversation on January 16, 1992). There is a cost sharing fee for similar services provided to existing congregations.

5

FACILITATORS

"And he gave some, apostles; and some, prophets; and some, evangelists; and some, pastors and teachers; For the perfecting of the saints, for the work of the ministry, for the edifying of the body of Christ" (Eph. 4:11-12).

As important as facilities are for a new congregation, the facilitators are more so. Everything rises and falls on leadership. It is absolutely imperative that the leaders of new work be God-appointed and God-anointed.

Those who are used of God to lead a new congregation must not merely be volunteers. They must be godsent and divinely commissioned. A divine call is essential to those who would set about to do divine work.

The Scriptures teach that God has specifically gifted certain persons to do certain tasks in the church. These are spiritual gifts, not merely innate attributes or skills. The anointing of God is a special touch for a specific task. So, at the proper moment and in the proper place, God especially equips certain ones to do the task at hand.

Apostles

Foremost among these especially equipped persons are the "apostles." Ephesians 4:11 says, "And he gave some [first], apostles." He also gifted some as "prophets," those called and commissioned to preach the gospel, and "evangelists," those especially equipped to evangelize, like our present-day evangelists that go from place to place and church to church leading evangelistic efforts. Of course, there are also some who are especially called and equipped of God to be "pastors," overseers who lead the church once established and shepherd the flock.

Some believe the office of "teacher" is linked to that of pastor, and thus they translate this verse, "and some pastor-teachers." Certainly the pastor does have an important teaching role, but I also believe God especially anoints and equips members of the body to serve with the pastor in the important role of teaching the Word of God and the doctrines of the faith. Again, probably no one should assume the role of teacher in a New Testament church who has not first prayerfully considered this important responsibility and felt a definite leadership of God, yes, even a calling of God to fulfill that task.

It has always amazed me that many well-trained public school teachers, who do an excellent job in their profession, sometimes fail as teachers within the body of the church. By the same token, literally thousands of Bible teachers serving in the church throughout the nation and around the world have no professional training whatsoever but are most effective teaching within the church. Of course, it is the gifting and enabling of the Holy Spirit, not professional training, that equips one to serve effectively as a member of the body.

But who are the apostles? Were they simply that small group of twelve who followed after our Lord while He was here on earth? Was Paul the only one serving in the apostolic role after Jesus and the twelve were gone? Most important of all, is there still an apostolic role in the church today? In these last days is God still calling, equipping, and sending forth His apostles?

Who is an apostle?—The word "apostle" comes from the Greek word *apostolos*. According to *Thayer's Greek-English Lexicon of the New Testament*, it means "one sent forth. . . ." What were these early biblical apostles sent forth to do? The Scriptures clearly indicate the biblical apostles were sent forth to evangelize and establish churches in places where churches were needed.

In his very thought-provoking book, *The Normal Christian Church Life*, Chinese evangelist Watchman Nee states, "The apostles were especially commissioned of God to found churches through the preaching of the gospel."[1]

In other words, in that early apostolic era, God raised up within the body certain ones He gifted and equipped to go into an area where a church was needed, evangelize the lost, and establish a congregation.

Probably the modern term "missionary" is the closest to the biblical concept of the apostle. However, these early New Testament missionaries (or apostles) were not sent out by a denomination or a missions agency or even a local church. First and foremost they were sent by God. It is imperative that today, even as then, those who go out to establish a new work be "sent by God."

Watchman Nee also makes the point that it is divine gifting and commission that equips one for apostleship, not just innate abilities and skills.

> The apostles were gifted men but their apostleship was not based upon their gifts, it was based upon their commission. Of course, God will not send anyone who is unequipped, but equipment does not constitute apostleship. It is futile for anyone to assume the office of an apostle simply because he thinks he has the needed gifts or ability. It takes more than mere gift and ability to constitute apostles; it takes God himself, His will, and His call. No man can attain to apostleship through natural or other qualifications. God must make him an apostle if he is ever to be one. "A man sent from God" should be the main characteristic of our entering upon His service.[2]

Further Watchman Nee quotes John 13:16 where Jesus said,

> The servant is not greater than his Lord neither the apostle (Greek) than He that sent him. Here we have the definition of the word "apostle." It implies being sent out—that is all and that is everything. However good human intention may be, it can never

take the place of divine commission. Today, those who have been sent out by the Lord to preach the gospel and to establish churches call themselves missionaries, not apostles, but the word missionary means the very same thing as apostle, i.e., "the sent one." I fail to see the reason why true sent ones of today prefer to call themselves "missionaries" rather than apostles.[3]

Perhaps it would be appropriate for modern-day missionaries to call themselves "apostles." After all, "evangelist," "prophet," "pastor," "teacher," and "deacon" are all biblical terms that have simply been transliterated into the English language. However, the modern misconception that the apostles were that select few whom Jesus Himself called forth and discipled might cause confusion in the minds of many. For people to call themselves apostles might suggest they considered themselves equals to the original twelve, "super saints" that are worthy of special reverence and respect.

Nevertheless, let the reader clearly understand, the role of the apostle is just as real today as in the first century and just as important to the church now as it was then. There are today, as in the days of the first century, those that God has especially raised up, called, equipped, and sent forth to evangelize and congregationalize areas where churches are desperately needed.

One of the great tragedies is that the role of the apostle is the ignored calling. Although most seminaries have very sophisticated training programs for those preparing for every other calling in the New Testament, most have very little, if any, training for the apostle. There are curriculum tracks to pursue for those who are planning to be pastors, ministers of education, ministers of music, evangelists, youth ministers, and recreation ministers. But what is there for those who have felt especially called of God to be church planters? How many seminaries have a major in church planting? Some have a course or two, but very few have a specialized and thorough program of training for those who have especially sensed the call of the apostle. This is an area of neglect in the Christian training centers of America in every denomination.

What are we to say to those who argue that the role of the apostle was confined to the original twelve, plus the apostle Paul, or at least to the New Testament era? They argue that with the passing of the first century and the canonization of the Scriptures, this New Testament office was eliminated and the role of the apostle ceased.

Let us study the Scriptures on this matter.

Indeed, Jesus did call and send forth the twelve who did merit and achieve special recognition by the early New Testament church and all followers of Christ since that day. They were not just called apostles, they were called the "twelve apostles." In fact, Jesus promised Peter that there would be a day when they would "sit on thrones judging the twelve tribes of Israel" (Luke 22:30).

However, it is important to note that when Judas betrayed the Lord, Matthias was chosen to be his successor and he also was "numbered with the eleven apostles" (Acts 1:26). In other words, Matthias was also considered an apostle.

These first twelve received a special place and honor in history. We are told in the Book of Revelation that in the new Jerusalem, "The wall of the city had twelve foundations, and in them the names of the twelve apostles of the Lamb" (21:14).

But this by no means ended the office, the role, or the calling of the apostles. Surely the gift of the "apostles" referred to in Ephesians 4:11 had no reference to these original twelve. These obviously are functioning offices within the church, even though Jesus Himself had already ascended.

Acts 14:4 tells us, "The multitude of the city was divided: and part held with the Jews, and part with the apostles." Who were these apostles that had been sent into Iconium to minister and establish a church there? They were Barnabas and Paul. Again, in verse 14, Paul and Barnabas are referred to as "the apostles." Neither Paul nor Barnabas were numbered among the original twelve, but they were definitely referred to as "apostles."

Watchman Nee states,

God appointed His son to be "the apostle;" Christ appointed His disciples to be "the twelve apostles;" and the Holy Spirit appointed a group of men, apart from the twelve to be the body building apostles. There are many belonging to this latter order chosen and sent forth by the Spirit of God.[4]

In 1 Corinthians 4:9 we read, "God hath set forth us the apostles last." So, we assume that in addition to Paul there were others who were apostles. A study of the Scripture indicates that there were at least two others with Paul when he wrote these words, namely Apollos (v. 6) and Sosthenes, Paul's scribe. Apparently the "us" refers either to Apollos or to Sosthenes or perhaps to both. In Romans 16:7 Paul refers to Andronicus and Junia as fellow prisoners who are "of note among the apostles." He does not mean that they are greatly admired by other apostles but rather that they are notable apostles themselves. None of them had ever seen Jesus, met Jesus, heard Him preach, or followed after Him, but even so they were "notable apostles," ones who had been sent forth by God to do the important work of ministry.

"We might have been burdensome, as the apostles of Christ," Paul writes in 1 Thessalonians 2:6. Certainly the "we" here refers clearly to the writers of this Thessalonican letter, namely, Paul, Silvanus, and Timothy. This indicates that not only Paul but also these two young fellow workers were "apostles."

Further, Paul states a very revealing thing in 1 Corinthians 15:5-7 when he says, "He was seen of Cephas, then of the twelve: After that, he was seen of above five hundred brethren at once. . . . After that, he was seen of James; then of all the apostles." Who was it then who had seen the risen Christ? The original apostles, plus 500 brethren at once, plus James, then by "all the apostles," that is all the apostles besides the original twelve who were alive at that time. You will recall that after Jesus had selected the original twelve and sent them out (Matt. 10:1-5), the Bible says Jesus sent out seventy others also (Luke 10:1). These, plus any others that may have been called and sent forth, shared with the original twelve in witnessing the risen Christ.

However, didn't Paul claim to be the last of the apostles? Didn't he say in 1 Corinthians 15:8-9, "Last of all he was seen of me also, . . . For I am the least of the apostles, that am not meet to be called an apostle." No, Paul did not say he was the "last apostle" but rather that he was "least" of the apostles. Had he been last, there would have been no others after him. But if so, why were there obviously others called and sent forth later and why did he instruct the church regarding the role of the apostle? (Eph. 4:11).

Long after all the original apostles had died and gone to heaven, with the exception of the apostle John, exiled on the island of Patmos, Jesus speaks to the angel of the Ephesian church, "Thou hast tried them which say they are apostles, and are not, and have found them liars" (Rev. 2:2). If there were only twelve apostles or even if Paul were the last of the apostles, who were these "apostles" who were tried by the church at Ephesus and found to be liars? If there was no longer a legitimate role of the apostle, surely no one would have purported to be one nor would there have been any need to "try" apostles to determine if they were legitimate.

It is obvious that the role of the apostle not only continued throughout the New Testament era but was a very vital and important function in the work of the church, particularly in the establishment and founding of new congregations. Certainly, it was well understood the body could not expand and grow nor could the Great Commission ever be fulfilled unless the role of the apostle was thoroughly recognized and acknowledged, prayed for and supported, and given highest honor and prominence. It is simply impossible to evangelize and congregationalize the world, as Jesus ordered in His Great Commission, apart from the functioning role of the apostle.

There is absolutely no hint in Scripture that this important office of the church has been eliminated. It would be just as logical to assume that the role of pastor, deacon, evangelist, prophet, or teacher is no longer legitimate. For the body to function effectively, it needs all its members.

Modern-day apostles.—Who then are the modern-day apostles? They are those who have been especially called by God and sent forth to establish new churches. They may or may not serve as pastor of the new congregation in its formative days, but they are the catalytic agents of God who, led by the Spirit, determine a field where a new work should be established and set about to "make it happen." After several months or years, when the work is firmly established, God may lead them to another place. Or, He may elect to change their role from "founder" to "developer." The same person who has served as apostle getting the work started may later sense God's call to continue as pastor for an indefinite period of time, developing the work and shepherding the flock. But it needs to be clearly understood at this point the biblical role has changed from "apostle" to something else. Once the work is firmly established, the role of the apostle is no longer valid in a local congregation.

Many years ago, Reverend Pat Brock sensed the call of the apostle even though he probably did not recognize it as such. Nevertheless, it was clear in his mind that God's will for his life was to establish churches, get them started, then move on to another place to found another congregation. Over a period of years he has been used of God to start twenty churches throughout Ohio, West Virginia, and Pennsylvania.

Likewise, Cornelius Bright gave his entire life and ministry to planting new churches throughout Ohio and Pennsylvania. When he died in 1985, he had helped begin sixty churches.

Reverend Benny Delmar has been used of God to start or help start over three hundred churches throughout the Northwest, mainly in Wyoming, Montana, and the Dakotas. Even though he is now seventy-three years old, he is still at it, pastoring a new work in Casper, Wyoming.

Some of our greatest and most effective modern-day apostles are women! Even though the Bible gives no examples of women pastors, it seems that then and now women are often very effectively used of God to begin new work.

Perhaps one of the greatest examples of a modern-day apostle is Tillie Burgin, minister of missions for the First Baptist Church of Arlington, Texas. Several times already in previous chapters I have referred to the First Baptist Church of Arlington with over one hundred satellite mission congregations meeting throughout the Arlington area. Every one of these was the direct result of Tillie Burgin's apostolic function. Even though she does not pastor any one of these satellite congregations, she has been instrumental in planning and establishing every one of them. She locates places where new work needs to be started, gains permission to use a facility, lines up the workers, trains those who will be leading the work, and coordinates the whole process of starting and developing at least one new mission congregation every month! I imagine she is one of the greatest church planters in history.

Dolores Thomas of Maine is another good example of a modern-day woman church planter. She and her husband went to Maine in 1962 to pastor a new congregation. For several years they ministered faithfully, establishing and growing that new church until her husband's untimely death in 1976. But Dolores did not quit or return defeated to her home in the South. She shared her husband's apostolic call and continued as a church planter, supported by the Home Mission Board and the Baptist Convention of New England. During these thirty years she has been responsible for starting fifteen churches.

Dottie Williamson, a Southern Baptist church planter in Mississippi, is another excellent example of a modern Priscilla, called of God and sent forth to evangelize and congregationalize communities where churches are needed. First in Virginia and now in Mississippi, she is a church planter par excellence beginning works, as God leads, wherever they are needed. She is emphatic in stating that she does not pastor these works nor does she preach at the Sunday morning worship services. Nevertheless, she is the chief agent of God, enlisting sponsoring churches, locating the "faithful few" to make up the nucleus for the new congregation, finding a place to meet, promoting and advertising the services, and scheduling preachers to speak at the worship services. God had used her mightily. She has been responsible for establishing five churches throughout Virginia and Mississippi.

My great-grandfather, Marcellus Whiteside was a nineteenth-century apostle who gave his adult life and ministry to starting new churches throughout the state of Missouri. He was never appointed, approved, commissioned, or subsidized by any missions agency. Nevertheless, as a young minister he strongly felt God's apostolic call and, as a bivocational minister, gave the rest of his life establishing Baptist churches in pioneer villages and rural areas. He is purported to have started over forty Baptist churches in Missouri, many of which still exist as small but thriving country and village churches.

Scores of laymen and laywomen have also sensed the call of the apostle. The Home Mission Board of the Southern Baptist Convention now has over fourteen hundred Mission Service Corps volunteers under appointment, many of them in one way or another assisting in the establishment of new churches throughout the nation. About one third of these people are retired and are responding to the missionary call, going as God leads to an area of need, working without salary or benefits from any agency or denomination, seeking only the reward of being faithful in God's service. God is calling and sending many of these volunteers to new Convention areas where Southern Baptist churches are few.

In many of these places it is difficult to find locally even the "frontier four," four families that will make up the nucleus of a new work. Praise God for those who will heed His call to go to one of those places and be one of those founding families. They may never pastor the work or preach in the pulpit, but their very presence will be a godsend and may mean the difference between life and death for the new mission. They will assist in its outreach and ministry in the community where it exists. They will provide leadership for the new work, teaching in Sunday School, assisting with the training program or the youth ministries, or even with the music program of the church. Their very presence becomes a conduit through which God's Spirit can flow to touch lives and bring souls to Christ.

Yes, God is definitely in the business of calling forward and sending forth His modern day apostles. May their tribe be multiplied throughout the earth.

Workers Needed in a New Congregation

Mission pastor.—Of course, the new work needs an undershepherd, one to lead and pastor the flock. In its inception, the church planter apostle may serve as pastor of the new work, if the Lord so leads and gifts him for that task. Of course, whoever serves as pastor needs to be elected both by the mission congregation and the sponsoring church. (The sponsoring church can elect and appoint someone to serve as pastor without the concurrence of the mission congregation, but in most cases it would not be wise to do so. The mission congregation cannot call a pastor without the approval of the sponsoring mother church.) A temporary or interim pastor may serve the new congregation. The director of missions or someone on the associational staff could serve in this capacity, or some other denominational worker from a state convention or a local Baptist institution such as a college or seminary. Many new congregations call ministerial students from a nearby college or seminary to pastor their work. Sometimes there is a retired pastor in the area or an ordained minister who is a member of one of the local churches who will serve, temporarily at least.

By properly arranging the times of worship services, the pastor of the sponsoring church can also serve as pastor of the new congregation. He may conduct Sunday morning worship services at the new mission at 9:00 or 9:30 a.m., returning to the mother church to conduct a worship service at 10:30 or 11:00 a.m.

I served churches for fourteen years that started at least one new mission every year. Most of the time I was pastoring both the mother church and the new mission, conducting services at both locations. On Sunday evenings, the new congregation usually joined the sponsoring church for worship. We conducted midweek services at the new mission, usually meeting in a member's home, on Tuesday evenings and at the mother church on Wednesday evening. On Tuesday afternoons and early evening I visited on the field of the new mission prior to the Tuesday evening worship service.

Of course, the ideal is for the new congregation to have a competent, full-time pastor from the outset. If the mission or the sponsoring church has the resources to fund a full-time pastor, they should not hesitate to do so! It is money well spent and will return rich dividends. Sometimes the state convention and the Home Mission Board will assist in funding a full-time pastor.

Musicians.—Music has always been a vital and important part of Christian worship. Even in biblical days psalms and hymns were part of every worship experience.

A good worship leader is important in the work of a new congregation. Hopefully, the Lord will raise up someone who can lead the congregation in experiencing meaningful worship through good quality sacred music. The type of music used should be carefully chosen so as to provide a pleasing and profitable experience for those who attend. In one place formal, almost liturgical music might be appropriate. However, in many other places this would be unappealing. Prayer choruses and hymns would be far more effective in fulfilling the objective of this church to reach people for Christ and develop them in their faith and witness.

Whatever music is chosen, it should communicate gospel truth and warm the hearts of the congregation. The purpose of the church music program is not to enhance the congregation's appreciation for fine classical music. Rather, it is to enhance the church's effort to evangelize the community by attracting residents to the worship service and blessing their hearts through the music provided.

In most cases, an instrumentalist is also needed. If a pianist and piano are available, this is an excellent asset to the worship service. However, in many places neither is available. Someone with a guitar leading the congregation in praise choruses and hymns may suffice just as well.

Baptist Book Stores and other Christian bookstores sell the Hymn Player® at a reasonable price, an electronic synthesizer that will play six hundred hymns and songs.[5] For some time chaplains have been using these instruments, even on the battlefields. Hymn Players are now used in many new congregations as well as they worship God through good gospel music.

Sunday School Workers

Not all new congregations will want or need a Sunday School with classes for all ages. Congregations in jails, retirement centers, parks, and elsewhere may not profit from a graded Sunday School. Some ethnic and black congregations are not familiar with Sunday School and may not sense the need for such an organization.

However, no matter how it may be organized, every congregation of new believers needs a Bible study program just like every new believer needs to be fed from the Word of God. Although much Bible is taught, or at least should be taught, from the pulpit of the church, still there is a need for in-depth Bible study by every member of every family, closely graded so that Bible study will be on the level of every student.

If no graded Sunday School is provided, where will the children and the youth get specific information for their own age? In most cases, it will not be adequately provided in the home and first and second graders will likely get very little quality Bible teaching simply by listening to the pastor.

But just as important as the teaching function of the Sunday School is its reaching responsibility. The Sunday School serves the church not only as an effective program for indepth teaching of the Bible but becomes the outreach agency for the new congregation.

Through a door-to-door or telephone survey, prospect cards or lists are made for every unsaved and unchurched person of every age in the church's community. These are assigned to Sunday School classes and the teachers of those units. Teachers must understand that they have a dual responsibility, "teaching" those who attend and "reaching" those who don't! They should dedicate at least two hours every week to preparing the Sunday morning Sunday School lesson but also commit at least two hours every week visiting the members enrolled in their class and those who are prospects for their class. If they are not willing to make this commitment and fulfill it faithfully, they should not be elected as teachers. The ability of the Sunday School to function in effective outreach as well as instruction demands dedicated workers who understand their dual role.

With few exceptions every new church should begin from the very first Sunday with a graded Sunday School led by God-appointed, anointed workers. As the church grows, and it surely will if these teachers are serving faithfully, new Sunday School classes should be started and additional workers involved. It is logical to assume that the more workers we have the more work will be done. The more people knocking on doors every week enlisting people for the Sunday School classes and departments, the faster the church will grow and more people will be reached for Christ. However, Sunday School teachers must be "workers" not "shirkers." Poor teachers who will not prepare adequately or visit regularly will destroy rather than build a class or department. Dedication and commitment in both teaching and outreach is imperative.

Whether the new congregation is Anglo, ethnic, or African-American, a top-quality, graded Bible teaching program should be started as soon as possible. It will become the backbone of the new work stabilizing it through the years.

Other Organizational Leaders

Other workers will be needed to staff the church's training program, mission organizations, etc. In many cases it will not only be possible but appropriate to start all of these organizations at the very outset. However, where workers are scarce or adequate space unavailable, it may be necessary to postpone the beginning of additional organizations until the work has developed more fully. In many cases it may never be possible to implement all the recommended organizations and programs, especially in satellite units or unique congregations. Denominational programs do not exist as an end in themselves. They are only suggested and provided as they appropriately meet the needs of a particular congregation. They should never be started simply to satisfy somebody's whim or to merely provide that which is "traditional." If they don't meet a need, we don't need them.

Ushers

It is important to have greeters at the door, meeting people as they arrive with a warm welcome and a friendly handshake. Ushers should assure order is maintained and disturbances eliminated. Ushers are necessary to pass the offering plates and safeguard the collection. Men, women, adults, or young people can serve adequately as ushers. In fact, one of the best ways to highlight youth and help them feel a part of the work is to assign them the ushering task. However, the ushers need to be trained and thoroughly instructed so they will perform this important function with dignity and grace. Sloppy ushering is offensive and may well be used of Satan to drive people away from the new congregation.

Deacons

The biblical office of the deacon is very important. However, it is not necessary for a new congregation to have deacons. In fact, it is probably wise to wait at least one year before any member is elected to this important office to avoid "laying on hands" hastily. Even if people have joined the new congregation who are already ordained deacons, it would probably be better to wait until they have proven themselves in the life of the new congregation before they are elected to active status.

Committees

Perhaps a good rule for committees in either a new congregation or an established church is simply "as many as necessary, but as few as possible." Countless committee meetings and taxing committee involvements often deter the members from the priority task of outreach and ministry. If members are required to be present for some committee meeting on Monday evening, then expected to be present for the midweek service on Wednesday evening, don't be surprised if they don't show up for visitation. If they have already spent several hours a week in committee assignments, it is doubtful that they will be out Saturday afternoon visiting their class members and prospects.

Probably a new congregation would be wise to have only one basic committee serving in several functions. A church council, composed of congregational leaders such as the music director, the Sunday School director, the director of the missions organizations, the person assigned to work with youth and, of course, the pastor, can form a coordinating committee that assumes nearly all the responsibilities necessary for a new congregation. They can meet once a month, discuss all matters relating to the church and its work, make appropriate reports and recommendations to the church, and thus free up themselves and the other members for the important witnessing and ministry task. That one council can serve as the missions committee, the evangelism committee, the baptism committee, the Lord's Supper committee, the music committee, etc., without taxing the time and energies of the entire membership with diverse committee assignments.

As the church grows and develops, it may be necessary to add additional committees, but it is still wise to follow the rule, "as many as necessary, but as few as possible."

Since New Testament days, God has raised up the leaders He needs for the work He has determined to be done. If God has truly led in the establishment of this new congregation, He will, no doubt, provide the leaders necessary to establish that work.

Perhaps with workers as well as finances we can claim the promise of Philippians 4:19, "My God shall supply all your need according to his riches in glory by Christ Jesus."

NOTES

1. Watchman Nee, *The Normal Christian Church Life,* rev. ed. (Washington, D.C.: International Students Press, 1969), 19.

2. Ibid., 17.

3. Ibid.

4. Ibid., 21.

5. The Hymn Player® (item number 4307-60) is also available from the Sunday School Board. Toll free ordering: 1-800-251-3225.

6

Funds

"Go your ways: behold, I send you forth as lambs among wolves. Carry neither purse, nor scrip, nor shoes" (Luke 10:3-4).

"My God shall supply all your need according to his riches in glory by Christ Jesus" (Phil. 4:19).

"Which of you, intending to build a tower, sitteth not down first, and counteth the cost, whether he hath sufficient to finish it?" (Luke 14:28).

As the Lord prepared to send out the seventy apostles to evangelize and start new churches, He instructed them to "Carry neither purse, nor scrip, nor shoes." He was simply reminding them that God would supply their needs if they would trust Him day by day and set about, as best they were able, to do that which He had sent them forth to do.

However, on another occasion He reminded His disciples of how foolish it would be to set about on some endeavor without having carefully considered the cost. He told them how foolish it would be to set about to build a tower without making an estimate of the cost, only to find that halfway through the project they would not have enough finances to complete the work. How foolish, He implied, to not carefully and prayerfully consider the cost.

Sometimes it seems to us that everything in the world depends on finances. Certainly, when planning to begin a new congregation, one must carefully and prayerfully consider the cost. Accurate estimates should be made of all anticipated expenses and a budget prepared with specific allocations for every anticipated cost.

There is a simple but important rule to follow in fiscal planning, "If you don't have it, you can't spend it." A church that spends money it doesn't have, incurring bills it cannot pay, inaugurating programs it cannot fund, borrowing money for land or buildings without sufficient resources to amortize the indebtedness, is certainly courting trouble. As someone has wisely said, "If your outgo is greater than your income, you are headed for a downfall."

As plans are made to begin a new mission, prayerful consideration must be given to finances. How will the salary of the pastor be paid? Where will we get the needed funds to purchase equipment and materials? How will we pay the rent on the facility?

A thorough budget needs to be planned beginning with a reasonable, conservative estimate of income. (See appendix, p. 156.) It is foolish to budget expenditures beyond income sufficient to meet those obligations.

Where does a new church get the funds necessary not only to begin this new work but also strengthen and expand its ministry?

Members of the Mission Congregation

The first source of funds should be the field itself. No new congregation should expect others to do for them that which they are able to do for themselves. As much as possible, the members should expect to "pay their own way" and not constantly be looking elsewhere for help.

God's plan to finance His work is very clear: "All the tithe of the land, . . . is the Lord's: it is holy unto the Lord" (Lev. 27:30). The proper stewardship of our possessions should be taught to all Christians, including the importance of the tithe being faithfully dedicated to God and His work.

The prophet Malachai reminds us that there is a blessing in store for those who are faithful in the stewardship of their possessions. "Bring ye all the tithes into the storehouse, that there may be meat in mine house, and prove me now herewith, saith the Lord of hosts, if I will not open you the windows of heaven, and pour you out a blessing" (Mal. 3:10).

God has never intended that His work be financed by bingo, rummage sales, or cakewalks! Such approaches are trite and unworthy. Rather, He orders the Christian to faithfully bring his tithe "that there may be meat in mine house."

Only after the members of the mission congregation have done their best as faithful stewards and found there is still not adequate funds to meet obligations, should they look elsewhere for financial assistance.

The Sponsoring Church

When parents give birth to a child, they naturally expect to pay the cost of delivery. From the outset they realize there will be a considerable price to pay. Having a baby and raising a child is expensive, but certainly more than worth the price.

Likewise, the church that sets about to birth a new baby congregation should expect to invest generously in this endeavor.

Churches often spend thousands and even millions of dollars on buildings and staff but sometimes flinch at investing even a small amount in starting and sustaining a new congregation. Yet, for the money spent, many more likely will be reached for Christ and discipled through church starting than anything else.

A Cosponsoring Church

Many times the primary sponsoring church of a new congregation is itself a small church with limited resources. Sometimes a cosponsoring church, perhaps even in another state, can be enlisted to give major funding to the new work. Also, the cosponsor may assist in other ways with witnessing teams, church builders, revivals, and Bible schools.

This concept has helped Southern Baptists for many years, especially in newer territories where most Southern Baptist churches are small and struggling financially. The local primary sponsor may be able to contribute several families to form the nucleus of the new work and give guidance and direction to its development. Unfortunately, they may not be able to give much if anything in financial support. A cosponsoring church with the resources to do so can be a godsend, providing much-needed financial aid.

The Roswell Street Baptist Church in Marietta, Georgia, was a cosponsor with the First Baptist Church in Las Vegas, Nevada, beginning the Southwest Mission in that area. For over three years, Roswell Street has contributed $1,000 per month to this new work and has seen it grow from about ten to over one hundred in attendance.

Assisting Churches

An assisting church is defined as any church anywhere that will give any amount to assist a new mission.

Sometimes a cluster of churches in a particular area or even an association of churches will combine their support to help start a new work. An association may lead in the establishment of the new work, and the churches of that association will provide the funding, either directly to the new mission or through the offices of the association. Usually one church is designated as a primary sponsor, but all the churches of that association or cluster will cooperate in providing financial support. Thus, the leader in founding the new congregation is not a mother church, but the association.

However, assisting churches may, like the cosponsor church, be far away as well as nearby. The home church of the pastor or a founding member may be interested in contributing to this new work. Churches the mission pastor has served previously are often interested. Members of the mission often have connections with churches where they were members at another time.

Discretion should always be used in approaching pastors or churches for support. Blanket mailouts are often offensive and seldom effective. High-pressure approaches should never be employed. Only with the full assurance of God's leadership should anyone approach a pastor or a church for support.

Your Denomination

The denomination exists to serve its churches and members. It has no greater purpose than assisting in the establishment of new churches in those places where they are needed.

The Home Mission Board is the major agency of the Southern Baptist Convention to assist in the funding of new mission congregations. In partnership with state conventions, salary subsidies may be provided for church planters and mission pastors in Anglo, ethnic, and African-American communities. Also, in many instances, the local association participates in providing an adequate salary and benefits for the mission pastor.

Unfortunately, resources are not sufficient to enable the Home Mission Board or the state conventions to assist every new congregation. In fact, only about one third of the church starts each year in the Southern Baptist Convention are assisted with salary supplements from the Home Mission Board. There are literally hundreds of places where new work is needed and where churches could be started if the finances were available.

In addition to providing salary subsidies, the Home Mission Board stands ready to help the new church in many ways. The Church Loans Division has site funds available so the new congregation can purchase property, providing they qualify for a loan. Up to $1 million is available to qualified borrowers for the construction of new buildings.

The Baptist Sunday School Board assists new Southern Baptist congregations in many ways. Twenty-five hymnals are given to a new congregation, along with Sunday School literature and other products. (See appendix, page 165.)

The Church Architecture Department of the Sunday School Board provides free architectural services to new churches, assisting them in designing attractive, functional buildings. They work closely with the church's planning and survey committee, construction committee, and architect in assuring that the new church gets the best building possible for their investment. (See appendix, page 169-72.)

State conventions provide invaluable services to new congregations. The state missions director and his staff are wise consultants, and their advice should be sought and carefully heeded. Usually there is a buildings consultant on staff who will work directly with a new Southern Baptist congregation advising them in the selection of a site and in the planning process for a new building. The pastor and members of a new congregation should seek the consultation and advice of their state convention staff.

Many state conventions have a foundation or special fund to assist new churches. This is another source where a new Southern Baptist congregation can turn for a site loan, a building loan, or, in some cases, salary assistance.

The Oldham Little Church Foundation (5177 Richmond Avenue, Suite 1068, Houston, Texas 77056) has been a godsend to many new, small churches. This foundation provides grants primarily for purchasing furniture and equipment for their new building.

Perhaps the greatest source of assistance Southern Baptists provide a new congregation is the local association and its staff. Any attempt to begin a new work should be communicated to the associational director of missions and his assistance should be sought. The work should be coordinated with the associational missions development council. The director of missions is a nearby help in time of need and should be involved at every step. His advice and counsel will be invaluable.

The Lord Himself

Fortunately, our dependence is not on a mission board, a denomination, or any human resource. The apostle Paul, one of the greatest church planters of all time, had a good word for churches today as well as to the church at Phillipi. "My God shall supply all your need according to his riches in glory by Christ Jesus" (Phil. 4:19).

God supplies our needs in many ways. Sometimes He supplies through a missions board or agency or from the support provided by a church, association, or state convention. Many times He supplies by providing employment, enabling us to serve as a bivocational "tentmaker," even as the apostle Paul himself. Sometimes the resources of the new congregation are sufficient, and there is no need to look elsewhere for funds.

No matter how He chooses to do it, He will "supply all your need." If He has led in the establishment of that new work, He will provide! He will not allow us to face an obstacle we cannot overcome or a need that He cannot meet.

When I went to Columbus, Ohio, as a church planter to begin the new Parsons Baptist Church, I was disheartened to learn that all Home Mission Board and state convention funds had already been appropriated, and I could expect no assistance from the denomination. The new mission congregation with only sixteen members could only provide twenty dollars per week in salary. However, the Lord soon opened a door of opportunity, and a local Southern Baptist church employed me on their staff. At the end of one year, Home Mission Board funds were available, and I did receive some salary subsidy but still worked one day a week teaching school as a substitute teacher. By the end of our third year, the new congregation was averaging over two hundred in attendance and was fully self-supporting.

"Thanks to be God, which giveth us the victory through our Lord Jesus Christ" (1 Cor. 15:57).

7

FELLOWSHIP MEETINGS

"And they continued stedfastly in the apostles' doctrine and fellowship" (Acts 2:42).

The early church began and continued in "fellowship meetings," generally held in homes. In most cases that is still the best way to begin a new church.

I have had the privilege of leading in the beginning of fourteen churches. Every one of these new church starts began with fellowship meetings in somebody's home. Beginning a church by meeting in somebody's home for prayer, Bible study, and worship is as ancient as the New Testament but as up-to-date as this morning's newspaper.

Why Have Fellowship Meetings?

The fellowship meetings might be compared to the gestation period for an unborn baby. Just as in childbirth, there needs to be a period of time for the new congregation to form, develop, and become as one. The fellowship meetings give prospective members a time to get to know one another, share their dreams, and become as one "body." Most important, it gives opportunity to determine if the Lord is really leading in the establishment of a new work at this time and in this place.

Who Attends the Fellowship Meetings?

All prospective members should be invited to attend the fellowship meetings. If there is a nucleus of member families in the sponsoring church interested in being part of the new work, they should be urged to attend. Perhaps members of other churches have indicated an interest. If so, they should be invited. It is hoped that a door-to-door survey has been made of the community and prospects have been discovered. They should be invited also. Usually the pastor of the sponsoring church will attend and will lead the fellowship meeting unless a mission pastor or church planter is already on the field. The director of missions for the local association should be invited, and in some cases will be chosen to lead the fellowship meetings.

Where Should the Fellowship Meetings Be Held?

Most of the time the fellowship meetings will be held in a home in the community where the new work will be located. It may be the home of a member of the sponsoring church or someone who was discovered during the door-to-door community survey or anyone else who may have indicated an interest. Sometimes the meetings will be held in different homes from week to week. However, it is probably better to stay in one location to avoid confusion.

How Long Should Fellowship Meetings Last?

Although it takes nine months to develop a human baby prior to birth, that ''gestation period'' may be a bit too long for a baby church. Probably the weekly fellowship meetings should continue not less than three months but in most cases not more than six months. They will meet weekly, usually on Monday, Tuesday, or Thursday evenings to avoid conflict with Wednesday evening midweek services, Sunday evening worship services, or Friday or Saturday family activities. However, in some instances they will meet Sunday evenings rather than a weekday. They should be one hour in duration, giving those who attend ample time to get home early enough for a good night's rest. It is good to serve refreshments and have a brief fellowship time following the meeting, but members should be free to leave whenever they choose. Avoid allowing the meetings to drag on, wearing out the members, and discouraging future attendance. It is important to begin promptly and close on time.

What Should Be Done in the Fellowship Meetings?

Among the important things to be done during the course of the fellowship meetings are the following:

Pray

The fellowship meetings give an opportunity for those interested in the new work to pray together for God's leadership and blessing. Every need should be brought before the Lord. A specific list of prayer concerns should be composed and ample time should be given for this time of prayer.

Plan

Plans have to be made and preparation has to be done as you consider beginning a new mission congregation. Where will this new work meet for worship and who will be in charge? Who will preach, lead the singing, usher, and who will open the building and have it ready for services? Who will teach the Sunday School classes, who will order the materials? Who will prepare a news release for the paper and who will send a circular letter to all prospects?

At least some of this planning can be done during the fellowship meeting.

Prepare

Having made detailed plans, job assignments should be made so that no detail will be neglected. During the fellowship meetings some time can be given to preparing the congregation for the first Sunday. It is important to "job check" every assignment to be sure nothing is left undone.

Have final arrangements been made for the facility? Has literature been ordered? Is the necessary equipment in place?

It is good to prepare a "checklist" of every conceivable task that needs to be done prior to the first meeting of the new mission. During the fellowship meeting, go over this checklist to be sure assignments have been made and are being fulfilled.

Preaching or Bible Study

At least twenty minutes of the hour should be devoted to a message or Bible study. Don't allow planning and preparation to dominate the entire hour, leaving no time for the members to be spiritually fed. Allowing for a discussion time, along with the Bible study, will do much to build camaraderie among the members. It is during this time with God's Word in the warm atmosphere of a home fellowship that the members will become as one in Christ.

Suppose after meeting for several months in weekly fellowship meetings, the group does not feel impressed to continue with the plans to begin a new mission. The group just hasn't jelled, and there is no strong desire to break ties with their present church or churches and begin a new work. They have enjoyed the fellowship meetings and getting to know one another but they do not sense God's leadership to launch a new work.

That is another reason why these fellowship meetings are so important. During this time God's will is revealed more clearly. If God is truly leading in the establishment of a new work in that place at that particular time, it will be made clear during these weekly meetings. It would be far better to discontinue the fellowship meetings and disband the group than to "pick green fruit" and attempt to launch work prematurely.

While I served on a state convention staff, my wife and I determined to help start a new church in our community. There was no Southern Baptist church in our immediate area, and the need seemed obvious. We did a door-to-door survey of our community and discovered a number of prospects. With the intention of beginning a new work, we hosted fellowship meetings in our home for several months. Everyone enjoyed the fellowship and the Bible study, and we formed friendship ties that continued for many years. However, as we discussed and planned toward starting a new church, there was little enthusiasm. It soon became obvious it was not the proper time to launch a new work. Several years later a new work was started in that area and continues to this day.

What is the difference between a fellowship meeting and a weekday evening worship service? Some congregations, especially indigenous satellite units or messianic fellowships, may choose to have their regular worship services on a weekday evening rather than on a Sunday morning. In fact, most messianic fellowship groups affiliated with the Southern Baptist Convention meet either on a Friday evening or a Saturday morning. Congregations that are part of a ministry center or congregations meeting in a college dormitory will often find it more advantageous and will reach more people for Christ and worship if they meet on a weekday evening rather than Sunday morning. Saddleback Valley Community Church in Mission Viejo, California, has one of their main worship services on Saturday evening.

Catholics have had mass on Saturday evenings for many years in some of their churches. Now many Baptist as well as other Protestant churches have found much greater success in reaching "baby boomers," "yuppies," and young adults, in general, with Saturday evening services.

From the outset, fellowship meetings, such as we have discussed in this chapter, are designed to prepare the congregation to later launch a new church-type mission. It is assumed from the beginning the fellowship meetings will not continue longer than six months and that a major portion of the time each week will be spent in planning and preparation for the new congregation, which in most cases will be meeting for worship and Bible study on a Sunday morning and perhaps a Sunday evening and midweek as well.

On the other hand, a congregation which has as its intention to meet on a weekday evening will have that as its objective from the very beginning. Their services will be devoted to Bible study and worship.

Do not discount the importance of weekly fellowship meetings preceding the launch of a new church. This appropriate gestation period is important, if not essential, for the beginning of most new work. Perhaps some indigenous satellite units could be established without this process. But most would be stronger and better if at least some time were spent in weekly meetings, praying, planning, and preparing for the establishment of the new congregation.

The Cell Group Phenomenon

Cell groups meeting in house churches have become a phenomenon in our day. However, in many ways this approach may be far more biblical than the traditional church meeting in worship centers constructed to house a large congregation. Yoido Full Gospel Church in Seoul, Korea, is probably the world's greatest example of the cell group approach.

The Yoido Full Gospel Church is not the only church in Korea using the cell group approach successfully. Nor has the successful use of the cell group approach been confined to Korea. House churches are spreading rapidly throughout London and other parts of Europe. There are also notable examples in Indonesia and various places in South America.

The cell group approach has proven successful in a limited number of places in the United States but has failed in others.

It is a mistake to study successful cell group methodology in Korea and conclude it will work equally as well anywhere and everywhere else. To do so is to court almost certain disaster. The culture is radically different. It is even more important to acknowledge the fervent, faithful prayer support Korean Christians give all their evangelistic, church-planting efforts.

Internationally known Korean pastor and evangelist Reverend Billy Kim cites five reasons he observes for the phenomenal growth of the Korean churches.[1]

Persecution.—For centuries, Koreans have been persecuted. As a mainland corridor between China and Japan, throughout the centuries Korea has been invaded and plundered from the north and from the south. Many times they have been conquered, their cities destroyed, and their people enslaved.

In more recent years, the atheistic communists of North Korea and Red China have sought to conquer their land. They have ravaged and plundered it time and again.

Persecution has driven Korean Christians to their knees. Like the blacksmith uses the fire to melt the metal, purge it, and shape it after his will, so has God used these times of persecution to shape Korean Christians into perhaps the most fervent, dedicated, committed colony of disciples anywhere on the earth.

Prayer.—Because of persecution and the continuing threat of invasion, fervent, effectual prayer has become a significant part of Korean church life. Nearly every Korean church, regardless of denomination, conducts prayer meetings every morning at 4:00 or 5:00 a.m., sometimes both. Literally thousands of Christians throughout Korea assemble daily at their churches for these early morning times of prayer, fervently praying for an hour or more before they proceed to their jobs.

Likewise, most of the churches have all-night prayer meetings every Friday. Christians in great numbers gather and spend the entire night in prayer, even though most Korean workers go to their jobs on Saturday as well as the other days of the week. They simply pray all night, go to their work, and claim they are just as refreshed and able as any other day.

Over thirty thousand people gather every Friday evening at the Yoido Full Gospel Church for the all-night meeting. The main sanctuary is filled to capacity with at least four or five overflow rooms where worshipers participate via close-circuit television.

When Koreans pray, they pray fervently! When the worship leader announces the time of prayer, they all pray out loud, at the same time, lifting their voices mightily unto the Lord. When the time of prayer is complete, the worship leader rings a bell and those in attendance cease praying.

To some observers this may seem like so much noise but to the Lord it is heavenly music indeed!

One wonders what would happen to American Christians and churches if large numbers gathered every morning at 4:00 or 5:00 a.m. for prayer? Suppose thousands of Baptists, Methodists, Presbyterians, and others decided to spend all night every Friday evening in prayer? Would we not also likely experience phenomenal growth as well as genuine revival and renewal?

Praise.—Another reason for the phenomenal growth of the work in Korea, according to Reverend Billy Kim, is the Korean Christian propensity to praise the Lord in all things.

Because of their persecution, Korean Christians have been driven to fervent prayer. God has answered their prayers by blessing them and their churches. They know full well these blessings come from the Lord in answer to specific prayers of faith. As a result, they praise Him continually.

Praise is not only contagious, it is magnetic. A Christian or a church filled with praise is attractive and appealing. People are drawn to such a person and to a praise-filled congregation.

The psalmist declares that the Lord "inhabitest the praises of Israel" (Ps. 22:3). When a congregation of God is filled with praise, the Lord is usually in that place in mighty power.

However, the converse of that is true as well. If the congregation is murmuring and complaining, disgruntled and defeated, Ichabod is written over the door, "The glory is departed" (1 Sam. 4:21). No matter how many ads we put in the paper, how many circulars we distribute, or how much promotion we do, people will stay away by the droves! Church should be a place for celebration and rejoicing and unless it is don't expect God to bless its ministry or that it will grow.

Proclamation.—According to Reverend Kim, proclaiming the gospel through preaching, teaching, and personal witness is the natural result of a Spirit-filled, overflowing life. Because Korean Christians have learned the power of prayer and praise, life-style witnessing is a natural.

Most Korean churches do not have visitation programs as such, with members gathering on a particular evening, receiving assignments, and going to an assigned home to bear personal witness. Maybe they should, and perhaps they would even be more greatly blessed if they did.

More typically, the Korean way is the way of the life-style witness, always ready to share their faith whenever opportunity avails. Most Korean Christians witness to others fervently and faithfully. They witness in the workplace and at the marketplace. But, most especially, they witness to their neighbors and friends.

This is probably why the house church is so effective. The Korean Christians are anxious to practice hospitality, inviting neighbors and friends into their homes, graciously hosting them, but also anxious for this opportunity to proclaim the gospel of the Lord Jesus Christ and bring these loved ones to a saving knowledge of God.

The Word does not return void. Thousands of Koreans come to know Jesus Christ every week as their Savior through the faithful, effective witness of their neighbors and relatives.

Propagation.—The Korean Church continually multiplies itself. Birthing new congregations is a way of life for the Koreans—not only through the starting of cell groups but also through the establishment of church-type missions. The number of congregations increase and multiply not only in Korea but throughout the world. Anyplace where Koreans settle, they start a church. That church, in turn, becomes a "launching pad" for other new congregations. In America alone the number of Southern Baptist Korean churches now exceeds seven hundred.

Dr. Ralph Neighbor, Southern Baptist pastor and former home missionary and church planter, has written an intriguing book entitled *Where Do We Go from Here?* Dr. Neighbor is convinced that traditional approaches to evangelizing and congregationalizing our nation and the world have not been successful in fulfilling the Great Commission. He is a fervent advocate of the cell group approach, not only in Korea or in Indonesia, where he has been copastor of a large cell group church, but in the entire world.

NOTE

1. Address by Reverend Billy Kim, International Conference of Itinerate Evangelists, Amsterdam, Holland, 1986.

8

FOUNDER'S DAY

"Upon this rock I will build my church; and the gates of hell shall not prevail against it. And I will give unto thee the keys of the kingdom of heaven: and whatsoever thou shalt bind on earth shall be bound in heaven: and whatsoever thou shalt loose on earth, shall be loosed in heaven" (Matt. 16:18-19).

Jesus was the first and greatest church planter. He is called "the Apostle" (Heb. 3:1). The church He established at Ceasarea Philippi was both local and universal. His promise that the "gates of hell shall not prevail against it" applies equally to the universal church and to the local church.

Proof that the church Jesus founded was local as well as universal is found in Matthew 18. Here Jesus advises His disciples, "If thy brother shall trespass against thee, go tell him his fault between thee and him alone: if he shall hear thee, thou has gained thy brother. But if he will not hear thee, then take with thee one or two more, that in the mouth of two or three witnesses every word shall be established. And if he shall neglect to hear them, tell it unto the church: but if he neglect to hear the church, let him be unto thee as an heathen man and publican" (vv. 15-17).

Obviously our Lord's reference here was to a local body of believers, not some vague, nebulous, invisible, or universal church.

There is a sense in which the biblical term for church (*ekklesia*) is used in a universal sense equated to the kingdom of God. Of course, when anyone receives Jesus Christ as Savior and is born into the kingdom, at that very moment he becomes part of the universal church. However, only seldom is *ekklesia* used in that sense in the Bible.

By far the predominant use of the word *church* throughout the New Testament is in reference to a local assembly. In fact, out of the 114 times the word is used, 95 refer to a specific, particular congregation or at least to the local church as an institution. These congregations were often small in number, were poor financially, had no church buildings or facilities; nevertheless, in the biblical sense, they were "church," the body of Jesus incarnate through His believers in that place. So, at least nine out of ten times, when the word *church* is used in the Bible, it refers to a local body, gathered for preaching, teaching, and worship, then scattered throughout the community to do in that place what Jesus would be doing if He were there physically. Endued and empowered by His Spirit, that local body duplicates and replicates His work in that place. "As my Father hath sent me, even so send I you" (John 20:21).

So there can be no more important historic day in the life of a new congregation than its birthday! As long as the church exists, its birthday must surely be considered its most memorable day. The gestation period is over, and the time has come for the baby to be born.

What are some things that should be done as we prepare for this great day?

Plan It Well

One reason for fellowship meetings is to give ample time and opportunity to plan this day well. There is much to be done and often very few people to do it. A checklist needs to be prepared with definite job assignments made to particular individuals. Someone (church planter, mission pastor, chairman of missions committee, etc.) should serve as coordinator, job-checking and assuring that assigned tasks are done.

The following are some of the important preparation items that should be accomplished before the new work begins.

Approval of the Mother Church

By this time it should be generally agreed by the pastor of the sponsoring church, the missions development committee, and members of the fellowship group that a new church should be established in this place. If so, members of the fellowship should request permission of the sponsoring church to begin services as a new mission congregation. If the missions development committee and the pastor agree, it should be recommended to the church for their approval. If the church approves, the mission congregation should proceed with plans to begin.

Bylaws Prepared

The missions development committee of the sponsoring church should prepare bylaws for the new congregation. These should include written guidelines relating to relationships and responsibilities between the sponsoring church and the chapel.

Among the items delineated in the bylaws should be:

1. The method whereby new members are received.

2. How money is received, deposited, and disbursed.

3. Business meetings and operations. (Until the new mission has constituted into a church, it has no authority to act apart from authorization from the sponsoring church. However, they may wish to conduct "recommendation services" in which they make recommendations to the sponsoring church for approval.)

4. Reports to the sponsoring church (i.e. financial reports, attendance reports). Usually there would be a weekly report submitted each Monday and a comprehensive monthly report at the end of each month.

5. The selection of a mission pastor and the election of officers and workers. Generally the missions development committee, with at least one representative from the mission serving on the

committee, serves as a pulpit committee in the selection of pastor and staff and as a nominating committee for the selection of the necessary workers.

6. Guidelines relating to the observance of baptism and the Lord's Supper.

Preparation of a Budget for the New Congregation

Working closely with the sponsoring church missions development committee, a well-planned budget should be prepared for the new mission. As much as possible, it should be clearly understood at the outset what amount will be contributed by the sponsoring church and how much is expected from the mission congregation itself. (See appendix for model budget.)

Enlist Needed Workers

As suggested in chapter 5, necessary workers must be enlisted and trained. These will include a preacher for the worship service, someone to play the piano or other musical instruments, someone to lead the singing, ushers, and teachers for the Sunday School classes. In addition, workers need to be enlisted to set up chairs and equipment and, following the services, to remove and store furniture and equipment.

Think of every item that needs to be done and be sure someone is specifically assigned to do it. If everybody thinks somebody will do it, probably nobody will.

Select an Appropriate Date

What is a good Sunday to begin a new work?

Some like to begin new mission congregations on Easter. More people are apt to go to church on this Sunday than on any other Sunday, and a new mission congregation in the community might prove attractive to many who do not regularly attend anywhere but are planning to do so on Easter.

Saddleback Valley Community Church in Mission Viejo, California, has started at least one and usually several new congregations every Easter for the past several years. Pastor Rick Warren feels this is the ideal Sunday to begin new work. They have started twenty new congregations over the past twelve years, and all of them were started on Easter.

Another good approach is to begin services with a "parent service" at the conclusion of a week of mission Bible school in the community. During the Bible school, many children from the community are enlisted; visits are made in homes; and parents are encouraged to attend the parent service on Sunday morning following VBS. This parent service becomes the first service of the new congregation.

A revival meeting can be used to launch a new work. The last Sunday of the revival can be the first Sunday of the new congregation.

Pray earnestly for God's leadership as you seek to determine the opportune time to begin the new work.

Promoting Founder's Day

Success of the first day of the new mission often depends on good promotion and good public relations. The following items should be done to assure that the first service of the new mission is communicated well to all prospective members.

Mailout to All Prospects

If a thorough door-to-door survey (or at least an effective telephone survey) has been made of all households in the community of the new mission and pertinent information has been tabulated on all prospects, a letter should be sent to all prospects announcing the date, location, and nature of the first service. In fact, a letter should be sent to prospects each week for several weeks prior to the beginning services. The letter should be printed, not mimeographed, and made as attractive as possible. Perhaps a circular or brochure advertising the first service with pictures of speakers and guests could be included.

Telephone Contact to All Prospects

During the week prior to the beginning of the new mission, there should be a telephone contact to all prospects. Inform them of the beginning services of the new mission, urge their attendance, and seek their agreement to participate.

If they indicate interest, consider assigning them a task such as assisting with setting up chairs and equipment, ushering, singing in the choir, or even bringing refreshments for the after-service fellowship time. Soliciting their involvement will do much to assure their attendance.

Personal Visits to Prospects

Did you hear about the soldier who sent a letter to his girlfriend every day for two years while he was in the service? He came home and discovered she had married the postman! A telephone call or letter cannot substitute for that personal visit.

Perhaps the sponsoring church, along with the fellowship group, could conduct a special visitation service on a particular weekday evening or Saturday prior to the beginning of the new congregation. Hopefully, every person on the prospect list could be visited the week prior to the beginning service. Appropriate materials could be given to the prospects, and an effective witness for Christ could be shared with every unsaved person.

"Pamphlet" the Community

The week prior to the beginning of a new work, an attractive circular advertising the first worship service of the new congregation should be left at every door in the community. Youth are excellent "pamphleteers." Mission groups also do well with this kind of project.

Ads in Local Newspapers

Attractive advertisements should be placed in local newspapers the week prior to beginning services, not only advertising the date and the times of the Sunday School and worship services, but also giving specific instructions as to the location. The ad needs to clearly identify when and where services will be conducted.[1]

News Releases

Well-prepared news releases should be submitted to all local newspapers, radio, and television stations in your community. The news release should be succinct, not preachy, and should answer the traditional reportorial questions of who, where, when, what, and why. A good-quality picture, perhaps of the mission pastor, speakers for the first service, special guests, or facility where the new church will be meeting should accompany the news releases. Most local newspapers will be happy to carry a good quality picture for a news event as significant as the beginning of a new church. Remember to invite the local religion reporter to the first service.

Attractive Sign

It may be possible to erect a large, attractive sign at the site of the new mission. However, since new congregations often meet in rented or leased facilities, frequently it is not possible to get the permission necessary to erect a permanent sign. However, a portable sign can often be prepared which can be transported to the site each week and set up prior to the services. This clearly identifies the location for those who are planning to attend and advertises the new church to the community.

In no case should a sign be prepared by an amateur who volunteers to do a sign in order to save the church some money.

Regardless of the cost, you should have a professional sign painter do this job so the new congregation will project the best possible image in the community from the very beginning.

The First Service

Do everything possible to make this first service a memorable event. Whether the attendance is large or small, it will always be remembered as the first service of the new congregation.

Outside Ushers

It is a good idea to have someone or even several people in the parking lot to meet people when they arrive. These outside ushers can direct people to a place to park, assist them out of their cars, and point them to the door. If it is raining, they could be there with an umbrella to assist people to the building or even park their car for them.

If you drive into the parking lot of a fine restaurant, there will probably be a parking attendant there to meet you, park your car for you, and show you to the door. Why shouldn't the church of the Lord Jesus Christ be as hospitable as local restaurants?

Greeters at Every Door

The mission pastor and members of the fellowship should be there at least fifteen minutes early, not only to assure that all furniture is in place and rooms prepared for Bible study, but also to be at every door, meeting people as they arrive. You never have a second chance to make a first impression! The first impression visitors receive when they arrive may well determine whether they decide to return. Nothing is more important to a new congregation than the evidence of a loving, caring, spirit.

Bible Study

Every Sunday school worker should arrive early to assure the room is prepared and everything is ready. They should be standing at the door to greet new students as they arrive.

The success of a new mission depends more on its spirit than on its building or facilities. People will travel many miles to worship and study the Bible in a place where they feel welcomed, wanted, and needed. A cold, indifferent spirit will kill any church, new or established. Certainly, the new congregation must do everything possible to communicate a spirit that says, "We need you! We want you! You are welcome in this place!" Someone has said, "People don't care how much we know until they know how much we care!"

Sunday School workers should be well prepared to present a Bible-based, needs-oriented Sunday School lesson. They should have spent at least two hours in preparation for presenting the lesson as well as at least two hours visiting members and prospects.

Well-planned Worship Service

Whether the worship service is more or less formal will, of course, depend on the community you are seeking to reach. "Context" is the key in determining the type service most appropriate.

Generally, Southern Baptists have found their best success with less formal worship services designed to warm the heart and bless the soul. The service should lead participants to worship and praise the Lord, not merely entertain or appeal to their aesthetic interests.

The first worship service might include a representative from the sponsoring church bringing a greeting from the mother church, as well as a statement authorizing the beginning of this new work. A member of the mission congregation might follow this greeting with a response and/or reading of the action of the fellowship group in requesting the sponsoring church to authorize the new mission.

The inclusion of special guests is always appropriate. Particularly, the director of missions for the local association, as well as the pastor of the sponsoring church, should be present to bring greetings. Of course, the chairman of the missions committee of the sponsoring church should be present. Sometimes the mayor of the city, or his representative or other community officials may wish to attend.

However, take care not to so completely fill the program with various people bringing greetings that no time is left for worship or the preaching of the Word. Those who attend need to feel they have been part of a genuine worship service and will want to attend again.

Of course, a definite invitation should be given, not only inviting the unsaved to receive Christ as Savior, but encouraging everyone present to join this new mission congregation. Those already involved in the fellowship meetings should come forward to pledge their commitment to the new mission even though they may already be members of the sponsoring church. Hopefully, others will be inspired to move their membership from whatever church they serve and become members of the new mission. Of course, until the new mission constitutes as a church, technically their membership is with the sponsoring church.

The following is a suggested agenda for the first service of a new Southern Baptist congregation:

Sample Founder's Day Worship Service
Prelude music
Opening hymn
Prayer
Welcome and recognition of guests
Greetings from the sponsoring church
    (Church missions development committee chairman and/or
    sponsoring church pastor brings greetings and affirms the

new congregation, assuring them of the sponsoring church's support.

Response from mission congregation (Someone from the mission congregation brings response, gives words of appreciation for the sponsoring church, and shares reasons why a new congregation is needed in that community.)

Greetings from other guests

Offertory hymn

Offering

Special music

Message

Invitation (Those present are invited to become members of the new mission)

Reception and fellowship

Recording the First Service

As long as the church lives, this in many ways will be its most historic day. Therefore, it is important to preserve the activities of the day for the historical record of the church.

Pictures and photos.—Have a photographer assigned to take pictures of those attending the first service. There needs to be top-quality photos of the preacher, those bringing greetings, various Sunday School classes in session, the worship service, and the fellowship time. It is important to assemble the entire congregation, perhaps in front of the building, for a picture. This is not only important for the historical record, but this picture will likely be a source of interest on anniversary services for years to come.

Taped recording and/or videotape of the services.—If possible, arrange to have both an audiotape and a videotape of the worship services. This should include the worship services from beginning to end, and interviews with those who are attending. The after-service reception is an excellent time to conduct these interviews.

News releases with pictures.—Immediately following the worship services, news releases should be prepared and taken to the local newspapers. Appropriate pictures should accompany the news releases. News releases should be hand delivered to the newsroom. Often the church page editor will be assigned to receive these releases and may wish to ask further questions regarding the event.

Suppose we do everything possible to plan this first service thoroughly, advertise and promote it as best we are able, and contact every known prospect only to discover very few or perhaps not even one person shows up for this first service? Even those who had been attending the fellowship and indicated interest in the new mission do not attend. Does this mean God is not in it and we should abandon the effort?

Not necessarily. That very thing has happened to many a church planter or mission pastor. After months of toil and preparation, many have seen their dreams shattered by a first service that appeared to be a total failure. When that final moment comes and ties with their mother church must be broken, sometimes even those who have been part of the fellowship group are not willing to make that break.

In times such as those, it is well for the church pastor to remember the words of our Lord, ''Where two or three are gathered together in my name, there am I in the midst of them'' (Matt. 18:20). It only takes a tiny seed to be the beginning of a giant tree! Often the first service of a new mission will be far more like that tiny seed than it will be like a giant oak or maple with spreading branches that everyone can see.

Many years ago a young pastor and his wife, right out of seminary, went to New Jersey to begin a new church. He worked faithfully for several months to prepare for the beginning of the new mission. He conducted fellowship meetings in a home for several weeks and advertised the first service of the new mission in every newspaper in the area. He delivered circulars to every door and, with the assistance of Home Mission Board summer missionaries, did a survey of the entire community. Letters were sent to all prospects advertising the first meeting of the new congregation.

He and his wife waited expectantly at the door for the first worshipers to arrive. Their excitement was great for numbers of people had indicated interest. You can imagine their disappointment when not a single person showed up at 9:30 a.m. for Bible study. Disheartened, they waited for the 11:00 a.m. worship service. "Surely, some will at least come for worship," they reasoned. However, 11:00 o'clock came and not a single person was present. The young pastor and his wife were not only disappointed, they were devastated. Their spirits were crushed. Holding hands, they sat together on the front row and began to weep. But even as they wept together, they heard the sound of someone entering the door. An elderly lady entered the building, greeted the pastor and his wife with these words, "For years I have been praying for a new church that preaches and teaches the Bible here in our community. At last my prayers have been answered! I am so glad you have come to help us start a new mission!"

The three of them composed the congregation for that first worship service. The pastor testified that he has never been so blessed in his entire ministry as on that first Sunday morning. They sang hymns, read the Scripture, took an offering, he preached and gave an invitation. The entire congregation, all three of them, joined the new mission that Sunday! Today, a thriving church ministers in that place.

God is and has always been in the church-starting business. Perhaps nothing is more important to our Lord than the beginning of a new congregation in a place where that body of Christ is needed. The work may begin large and strong or it may begin small and weak, but we must never despise the day of small things. Thank God for those who are giving themselves to the task of the modern-day apostle, birthing new congregations where they are needed throughout the world.

NOTE

1. For help in preparing advertisements, news releases, and other promotional materials see Wayne Kiser, *Promotion Strategies for the Local Church* (Nashville: Broadman Press, 1992).

9

FOLLOW-UP

"And they, continuing daily with one accord in the temple, and breaking bread from house to house, did eat their meat with gladness and singleness of heart, Praising God, and having favor with all the people. And the Lord added to the church daily such as should be saved" (Acts 2:46-47).

New Testament Principles

Five principles guided the early New Testament church as it sought to minister to its community.

The Principle of Involvement

Acts 2:46 says, *"They,* continuing daily with one accord." This implies all of them, not merely the apostles, participated in that new church's witness and ministry. There was no division of labor wherein members turned the responsibility of ministry over to a select few, such as the pastor and staff. They were all excited about their new church, and they were all heavily burdened for their lost community. They shared the responsibility of witnessing and ministering and realized sharing the load was everybody's task.

The Principle of Persistence

Likewise, Acts 2:46 says, "They, *continuing* daily with one accord." Oftentimes, members of a new mission will be excited about starting the new work, will attend the fellowship meetings regularly, will enthusiastically participate in the planning, and will be present for the launch day. However, when the new wears off and the mission is established, their enthusiasm wanes. Some may drop out altogether. They are excited about getting something going but not nearly so enthused about continuing it. Once started, if it doesn't meet all their expectations or if it doesn't grow as rapidly as they fancy it should, they drop by the wayside. Many times their expectations are unreasonable and their commitment is shallow.

It is good to remember the words of our Lord, "No man, having put his hand to the plow, and looking back, is fit for the kingdom of God" (Luke 9:62). Oldtimers sometimes say, "God has little use for a quitter." If something is worth starting, it's worth continuing and completing. Members of the new mission should be determined from the outset to continue faithful until they die, or until Jesus comes, or at least until He very definitely and specifically leads them to another place of service. You don't quit on God's work just because you are discouraged or disheartened.

The principle of persistence is never more important than in founding a new church.

The Principle of Daily Discipline

It is interesting to note in Acts 2:46 that they (the members of this new work), were "continuing *daily* in the temple, and breaking bread from house to house, . . . Praising God and having favor with all the people." It is also important to notice that as a result "the Lord added to the church *daily* such as should be saved."

In other words, the members of this new church were witnessing to lost people every day and, as a result, people were being saved every day. Since the Bible says these new converts were being added to the church daily, we conclude that they were not only witnessing to the lost but baptizing new converts into the membership of the church every day.

In our time, if a church has converts every Sunday and baptizes people every week we reckon that a great thing. However, because of the fervency and effectiveness of its witness, this first New Testament church was winning, baptizing, and discipling new converts every single day!

And this was all being done in a most unlikely church field. Probably at least 90 percent of the population of Jerusalem were orthodox Jews. This is the same city where the religious leaders had just a few weeks prior to this crucified Jesus on the cross. Not only the leaders but the large crowd gathered in Pilate's courtyard, participated in His condemnation and called for His crucifixion. Many of these same leaders and some of this same crowd that crucified Jesus had now been saved and baptized into the membership of this new church (Acts 2:36).

Could there ever be any harder place to start a new church than Jerusalem? Yet, because of the faithful witnessing of God's people, anointed by the power of God's Spirit, great blessing came even in this most unlikely place.

An effective mission pastor will discipline himself to giving several hours every day to visitation and witnessing to the lost. As much as they are able, at work, at school, in the marketplace, and with their neighbors and friends, and elsewhere, the members of the new mission will seek every day to witness for Christ and to invite people to the services of the new mission.

A scheduled time for weekly visitation is important and as much as possible every member of the mission should participate. But in addition to this, members should develop the art of "life-style witnessing," simply allowing the Holy Spirit to lead them and use them in sharing Christ wherever they are, as the Spirit leads. "Daily discipline" in witnessing and ministering in

Jesus' name by all the members of the new congregation is essential if the church is to make the greatest impact for Christ possible in the place where it exists.

The Principle of Saturation Evangelism

Acts 2:46 says they went "house to house." This may mean they went from one home to another, visiting fellow members and unsaved friends and relatives. All of them had kinfolk and friends that needed to know the good news that Jesus was the Messiah, the Son of God who had died on the cross for their sins. They boldly shared their testimony with these neighbors and friends, beginning with what we might call "relationship evangelism."

W. Oscar Thompson, Jr., in his book, *Concentric Circles of Concern*, expresses the importance of this type of cultivative evangelism beginning with our own immediate family and kin, then spreading out to a wider circle of acquaintances and friends. Generally, our influence and witness will be most effective with those we love the most and know the best.

However, there is ample evidence that this early New Testament church saw as its ultimate goal to share the story of salvation with every home, door to door, until they had, in fact, fulfilled our Lord's command to share the gospel with every creature (Mark 16:15). Apparently they determined, as their basic strategy, to see to it that a gospel witness was shared with every household in Jerusalem (Acts 5:42; 8:4). As a result, "The Word of God grew and multiplied" (12:24).

As the scope of Christianity was broadened and new churches were established throughout the area, this principle of "house-to-house" saturation evangelism, with its objective of sharing Christ in every home and with every person, continued (20:20, 31). As a result, the early New Testament church, even in an alien, hostile, environment was able to evangelize its community more effectively than any Church has ever done since.

The Principle of Genuine, Spirit-Filled Worship

As they went from "house to house," notice the Bible says they went "Praising God, and having favor with all the people" (2:47). It was surely this spirit of praise and rejoicing that made their testimony so believable and effective. Their witness was attractive, even to total unbelievers, because it was anointed with Spirit-filled praise.

A carnal Christian will never be an effective witness no matter how hard he tries. He can participate in every training program imaginable but until he witnesses from the overflow of a praise-filled life, his efforts will seem shallow and ineffectual.

What is true of the individual Christian is also true of the church. Not only in their personal witness but in their corporate worship, they were a praising people. Their worship service was a celebration, not merely a liturgy or formality. The very presence of the Lord filled the place where they gathered and one could, no doubt, feel His presence the moment one stepped through the door (v. 2). Even though they did not have fine buildings in which to meet and, more often than not, were simply meeting in some member's home, the presence of the Lord was in that place, and they were mightily and wonderfully blessed.

A new congregation, no matter where it may be meeting, will do well to adhere to these basic New Testament principles as it seeks to establish and develop a witness and ministry in its community.

A Letter to Everyone Who Attended

A letter should be sent to everyone who attended the first service, thanking them for participating in this historic day and urging their continued attendance. The letter should explain the need for a new congregation in that community and the need for them to be involved.

A different letter should be sent to those who came forward to join the new mission. Every week a letter of welcome should be sent to new members (See appendix, p. 166).

A Personal Visit to All Who Attended the First Service

Not only a letter but a personal visit should be made to everybody who attended this first service. Those who joined the new mission congregation should be given a packet of new member materials including the church's bylaws, the statement of faith, (i.e. *The Baptist Faith and Message* pamphlet for Southern Baptists), and other pertinent materials.

Those attending who did not join should receive a visit and also a packet of pertinent materials regarding the new church. Of course, the person making the visit will want to urge them to move their membership to the new congregation or, if they are unsaved, to share the plan of salvation as the Lord leads.

Prospect Cards

On the first Sunday, registration cards should be given to every person present. For those who didn't join the new mission, this information should be transferred to prospect cards which go into the church's prospect file. A prospect card should be made on every member of the family, not just the adults. Sunday School teachers in the children's, youth, and adult classes will need prospect cards for those who are of their particular age group.

On all following Sundays, visitor cards should be given to everyone who is not already a member. These people become the best prospects the new mission has as it seeks to witness effectively to its community. It is better for ushers to lose money out of the offering plate than to lose the visitor cards. This is vital information and should be followed up by visitation teams immediately.

A Weekly Newsletter

If possible, it is good to have a weekly newsletter from the new church sent every week for at least six months to all members and prospects of the new mission. This continuing contact with members, those who have attended, and other prospects will assist greatly in the efforts to establish this new work.

After six months or so it may be necessary to reduce the number of times the newsletter is sent from weekly to monthly. However, it is important to have at least a monthly newsletter going to both members and prospects.

Involve Every Member

"If we don't use them, we lose them." People are far more apt to be faithful and continue faithfully if they have a responsibility, providing they are not assigned more than they are reasonably able to bear. An "overload" may lead to frustration and a sense of failure and may cause the member to drop by the wayside. However, a responsibility commensurate with ability and interest will have just the opposite effect. Generally, people will be more faithful, study their Bible more seriously, and grow more rapidly in Christ if they have a meaningful, fulfilling responsibility.

A closely graded Sunday School provides an excellent opportunity for utilizing the talents and skills of the members in meaningful service. The church's training program and mission education programs also give excellent avenues of service.

Some who are not qualified or who don't want to teach can find important places of service. Setting up chairs and equipment, ushering, singing in the choir or assisting with the music, taking care of the building or grounds, or driving a church bus or van give opportunities for meaningful service.

Some may wish to be a member of the church's "Martha Club," a group of ladies (or men) who prepare meals and/or refreshments for church events.

It is good to fill out a survey card on every new member to determine their skills and interests in a particular area of service.

If people are interested enough in a church to join it, they are probably interested enough to serve in some meaningful way if given the opportunity. It is the church's responsibility not only to find people for every place of service but also to find a place of service for every member. The Bible says each of us must someday "stand before the judgment seat of Christ" and "to give account of himself unto God" (Rom. 14:10). God expects all of us to be faithful in His service and ministering through our church is one way we fulfill that divine expectation.

True, there are some, perhaps many, who simply do not wish to serve and will not do so no matter what the challenge. Some have called this the "me generation," with many not interested in serving others or making long-term commitments. If so, that is certainly contrary to the challenge of the New Testament and is a fault the church needs to correct, as much as possible. We must never compromise the New Testament's high standards in our call to commitment and service. "Everybody a minister" is the New Testament norm and should be the expectation of the church today.

Most people respond better to a challenge than they do to a compromise. Efforts to "market the church" by determining the whims and wishes of the population, then doing whatever necessary to accommodate those whims in order to attract numbers, is unworthy and unbiblical. The church is to be a prophetic voice in its community, denouncing sin, calling people to repentance, and challenging its members to ministry and service. Ours is not a gospel that can be watered down to meet the fancies of the crowd.

Expand the Structure

If the new church is to grow, its skeleton should grow. Nearly everything grows in proportion to its skeleton.

The skeleton of a strong church is its organizational structure. An expanding Sunday School continuing to add new classes and departments with the expectation of reaching new prospects is a time-proven outreach method. The Sunday School workers are outreach agents seeking to enlist every known prospect in their assigned age group. New and additional bus routes for the church that has a bus or van ministry will usually enlist an ever-increasing number of riders.

The church's discipleship program needs to keep pace with the need to disciple new members, train workers, and continue developing the members already enlisted. New member training, old member training, and leader training are three primary objectives of this program.

What can be more important to a church, new or old, or to the kingdom than an effective program to lead the church in mission education, mission support, and mission involvement?

Nearly anything works better organized than disorganized. Every church in the context of its own community and in respect to its own goals has to determine what organizations will best fit its needs and equip members to better do their task. Yet, its hard to imagine any church, whether Anglo, ethnic, or African-American, that does not need a quality Bible-teaching program for adult members and for the children and youth.

Likewise, it's hard to imagine that any church anywhere does not need some kind of program to train members to serve the Lord effectively, to understand the history and doctrines of their denomination, and to deal with the critical moral and social issues of our day. Certainly, those saved need to be discipled, and effective discipling does not happen by accident. If it's done, there has to be a plan and a program.

Programs and materials provided by the Baptist Sunday School Board in Nashville, Tennessee, for Bible teaching and training are among the very best. The church that does not use these materials is cheating itself and its members.

The Baptist Brotherhood Commission in Memphis, Tennessee, and the Woman's Missionary Union in Birmingham, Alabama, provide the necessary study materials, training materials, and literature for an excellent missions education program in the church regardless of its size. Probably most new churches, if not all, should have Brotherhood and WMU with their missions education programs for both children and adults.

Systematic Visitation and Witnessing

Sharing Christ with every person in its community should be the goal of every new church. To achieve this all members, not just the pastor, must participate in the church's witnessing task. This cannot be achieved by simply having worship services every Sunday and advertising that everyone in the community is welcome. The church must go beyond this, taking the gospel to the homes of the people through an active visitation and witnessing program.

The following are some approaches to visitation and witnessing that may prove effective:

The pastor's visitation and witnessing ministry.—If the new church is blessed with a full-time pastor, he should expect to spend at least fifteen hours every week visiting in the homes of members and witnessing to the lost. Above all else the pastor of a new church should be a soul-winner. He should have a heavy burden for the unsaved and work tirelessly to reach people for Christ.

The pastor needs to have an up-to-date prospect file with the names of every unsaved and unchurched person in his community. He should be regularly visiting these prospects, cultivating a friendship and, as the Lord leads, sharing the plan of salvation—challenging them to receive Jesus as Savior. He needs to have ample training so he is personally able to share the plan of salvation effectively and "draw the net." Likewise, he needs to be training his members to be soul winners also.

A pastor in Indiana has a simple goal to make five visits per day at least five days every week. Every day, Monday through Thursday, he comes to his office about 8:00 a.m., studies and does administrative duties until about 2:00 p.m., then visits until 5:30 p.m. He also goes out with evangelism teams every

Thursday evening, thus at least five visits a day, five days a week.

Another pastor has as his goal dividing his week into four segments of fifteen hours each. He spends no more than fifteen hours a week in his office doing administrative duties, another fifteen hours in his study preparing sermons and Bible studies, and allows fifteen hours for attendance at the regular meetings of the church, such as worship services, Sunday School, Discipleship Training, committee meetings, associational meetings, state convention events, etc. (He points out that many of these he would be doing anyway as a member of the church, even if he were not the pastor.) But he allows at least fifteen hours every week, and hopefully more, to visitation and soul winning. He claims that very seldom does he walk into the pulpit to preach on a Sunday morning without somebody being there that he witnessed to the previous week and often has already prayed to receive Jesus and is ready to make a public decision.

Further, this pastor claims nothing does more for his preaching ministry than the hours he spends talking to people personally about the Lord. He claims that an hour of soul winning does even more for his preaching than an hour of studying will do.

Some people argue that it's not the pastor's responsibility to visit and win souls, but rather that of the congregation itself. As one pastor put it, "Shepherds don't produce sheep, sheep produce sheep." He implied that the shepherd should spend his time doing administration and preparing sermons and let the members do the visitation and soul-winning.

Of course, this pastor failed to realize a very obvious truth. It is unlikely that the sheep will go anywhere that the shepherd doesn't lead them, except to go astray. If deacons are to be soul winners, Sunday School teachers are to spend several hours a week visiting and witnessing, and the members are to be actively sharing their faith, they need to see their pastor modeling a witnessing life.

As the pastor spends many hours witnessing to the unsaved and the unchurched, he is wise to take church leaders with him providing on-the-job training for deacons, Sunday School teachers, dedicated laypersons, and others. This way his time and energy will have double results, winning lost souls and, at the same time, equipping others to be effective in sharing their faith.

Churchwide visitation and witnessing.—From the beginning the church should have an evangelism program involving the members in the church's outreach task. The church may sponsor a weekly visitation session, perhaps following the Wednesday evening midweek service. Members may gather for prayer meeting and Bible study at 6:30 or 7:00 p.m., followed by visitation from 7:30 or 8:00 until no later than 9:00 p.m., then return to the church for reports.

A more typical approach is to designate either Monday, Tuesday, or Thursday evenings for visitation and witnessing. Members gather at 7:00 p.m., receive visitation assignments, visit for about two hours, then return to the church for reports. Some churches have a visitation supper prior to the session.

Women's visitation.—In some places, women's visitation is scheduled on a weekday morning, usually gathering at 10:00 a.m. for assignments, then returning about noon for a fellowship luncheon and report time. Since many women work outside their homes, this type of visitation may or may not be effective in particular settings.

It is usually a good idea to have child care provided for women's visitation. Then young mothers can bring their children to the child-care program, enjoy a fulfilling morning witnessing with a visitation partner, and return for a good time of fellowship at the visitation luncheon. Sometimes they bring those they have visited to the luncheon.

If this type program will not work on a weekday, you might consider trying it on a Saturday morning or afternoon.

Sunday School workers' visitation.—Some churches schedule Sunday School workers' visitation once a month on a Saturday morning, insisting that all Sunday School workers be present with a special effort to "blitz" every known prospect for every Sunday School class and department.

They meet at 9:30 a.m. on Saturday morning for refreshments and assignments and then visit from 10:00 a.m. until 12:00 or 12:30 p.m. Since they are visiting prospects for their own classes, they do not return for a report time.

Youth visitation.—Young people meet at the church one evening each week or each month for "vis-rec." They receive assignments of unsaved and/or unchurched young people in the community, go in teams of three or more to visit prospects, then return—with the prospect, if possible—for a time of refreshments and recreation. To add some interest, you might call the visitation teams "roundup teams" with their objective being to "round up" these unsaved and unchurched young people and "bring them back alive" for refreshment and recreation. This approach also works well during revival meetings.

Specialized outreach programs.—Continuing Witness Training (CWT), along with other programs like Evangelism Explosion, has proven successful in training members of new missions to witness effectively and in directing their soul-winning efforts. Usually led by the pastor, who has taken the witness training and is prepared to lead others, a small group is enlisted for thirteen weeks of training and directed visitation. Those who complete the thirteen weeks are then equippers and are used to train others during the next session. Thus, through a process of geometric progression, the number of trained witnesses multiplies as sessions are continued. CWT has become the "flagship" witness training program among Southern Baptists.

However, the Evangelism Section of the Home Mission Board now offers several optional approaches which can also be used effectively. The One Day Soul-Winning Workshop and the WIN School are designed to train people to witness using a simple witnessing booklet. The witness can share the plan of salvation with unsaved people by simply reading through the booklet with them and, if they desire, leading them in a sinner's prayer receiving Christ as their personal Savior.

Using whatever approach seems most appropriate, every new church should develop a plan to train and equip its members to witness effectively to the unsaved in their community. Witnessing to the unsaved is a mandate of the Great Commission. We can never claim to be a true New Testament church until members of the church are involved in reaching their community for Christ.

Constitute as a New Church

All parents hope and pray that their baby will some day be old enough and grow strong enough to be on her own. At that point children will likely leave home, get a job, make their own way, and perhaps marry and begin making plans to have their own children.

Likewise, it is hoped that this new church will grow and become ever stronger, and, at last, able to make it on its own without further nurturing and nourishing from the mother church. At that point, it is only appropriate that the mission request the mother church to allow them to constitute and become an independent congregation, no longer a mission of the sponsoring church. However, in their desire to be fully constituted and no longer dependent on the sponsoring church, new congregations often prematurely request the privilege long before they are ready for self-governance and self-support. Even though they may not realize it, they still need the direction and guidance as well as the support of the mother church.

Before a new church elects to constitute or before the sponsoring church agrees, the following questions need to be answered satisfactorily:

Has a unity of spirit and purpose developed in the new congregation?—Have they truly become "one in Christ?" Do the members see themselves as a functioning "body" strong enough to carry on the work of ministry without support or direction from a sponsoring congregation?

Is the new church doctrinally sound and fully in accord with the theological tenets of their denomination?—In the case of a Southern Baptist congregation, are the leaders and members in full agreement with *The Baptist Faith and Message* statement of faith? Is there any indication that if left on their own without the guidance of a sponsoring church, they might follow some theological tangent, assuming a doctrinal posture that is unsound and unacceptable among sister churches?

Is the church large enough numerically and strong enough financially to continue an effective ministry in their community?—It is not only a matter of their ability to pay their bills and sustain their present program, but it is also important that they be able to witness effectively and minister to the needs of their area. Do they have sufficient resources to achieve this without financial support from other sources?

Probably a new congregation should have at last one hundred faithful, resident members before it considers constituting as a church. However, in underprivileged areas where resources are scant and salaries are low, it may be important to have more than one hundred members.

Many congregations, especially satellite units, will likely never have the numerical or financial strength necessary to constitute as separate congregations. They may be dependent upon a sponsoring church for financial support, as well as for guidance, as long as they exist.

Satellite units are established with the intention that they will continue indefinitely simply as an arm of the meeting church, perhaps always dependent on the sponsor for financial support and direction.

Nevertheless, if these congregations represent groups of believers who are meeting weekly for Bible study, preaching, and worship, and then seeking, as best they can, to be an effective witness in their community, they are just as much "church" in the biblical sense as a fully self-supporting congregation meeting in their own building. Those attending the worship services may even be more greatly blessed than others attending a large church. In fact, they may be doing a far better job than many large, strong churches in ministering to the needs of their particular community.

We may be surprised, however, to see how rapidly many of

these new units grow and how quickly they reach a level of self-support. New churches started in the most unlikely situations often outpace others in their growth and effectiveness.

Southern Baptists have started many new congregations in ethnic or African-American communities thinking they would always need to be helped and subsidized by the sponsoring church and the denomination. Often, members of the mother church and denominational representatives are gladly surprised to see these become some of the fastest-growing churches and sometimes even the largest Southern Baptist churches in the area. Praise the Lord! Only He knows the final result when a new church is birthed in a particular community.

Other congregations may constitute and become bona fide New Testament churches. However, they may never be able to support a full-time pastor. They may be served by a bivocational or retired pastor but are self-sustaining with no support from other churches. Of the 37,000 plus constituted SBC churches, at least 10,000 are in this category. Many more are needed across America. These churches need to be affirmed. They are a vital part of "churching America." They are truly indigenous to their setting and people groups.

When the pastor of the mission, along with the mission congregation, agrees that the time is right for the mission to constitute, no longer looking to the church or the denomination for financial assistance (except perhaps for a loan to buy property or build a building), members should inform the pastor of the sponsoring church and the chairman of the missions development committee.

If the pastor of the sponsoring church and the missions development committee agree, the following steps should be followed:

1. The pastor of the mission congregation, or a representative of the congregation acting on behalf of the mission, should write a letter to the mother church requesting permission to constitute. The letter should be addressed to the chairman of the missions development committee with a copy sent to the pastor.

2. If the missions development committee agrees that the time is right for the mission to constitute, they should bring a recom-

mendation to the sponsoring church that the mission be constituted.

3. If the sponsoring church concurs with the recommendation and approves the constituting of the new church, an appropriate date should be set for the constitution service. Members of the churches of that association should be invited to participate along with appropriate denominational officials.

4. A committee should be appointed to write a constitution and bylaws for the new congregation. Of course, the pastor of the new congregation and other representatives should work with this committee, but the sponsoring church should take the initiative in preparing the documents.[1]

5. A letter of invitation, including copies of the constitution and bylaws, should be sent to appropriate denominational officials and to sister churches in the area inviting them to participate in the constitution service.

At least one hour prior to the constitution service, a council of pastors and ordained deacons from sister churches should be convened to review the constitution and bylaws, make any suggestions, and share any concerns. Hopefully, this council will look with favor on the constituting of this new congregation and, with appropriate revisions, will recommend to the group gathered for the constitution service that they proceed with constituting the new church.

To avoid any possible embarrassment or delay in plans, it is sometimes advisable to form this council several weeks prior to the scheduled constitution service. This could be prior to or after a regular meeting of the associational pastors' conference, executive committee, or some other associational event.

A council of this kind does not have the authority to order the church either to constitute or to refrain from constituting the new mission. But if the new church expects to be affiliated with the association, it is wise to have the approval of representatives from the association.

Like the birthday of the new congregation, the constitution service is a great and historic occasion. Every effort should be made to commemorate it.

Many of the same steps followed in preparing for the first Sunday of the new mission should be observed when planning and promoting the constitution service. News releases with pictures of speakers and special guests should be given to all the local newspapers, radio and television stations.

Special guests, including representatives of the mother church, the association, the state convention, and the Home Mission Board may be included.

Reporters from local newspapers may want to be present or, at least, somebody should be designated to record the activities of the day and prepare news release for the media.

Both audio and videotapes should record the service from beginning to end for the church's historical archives. The service should be a fitting tribute to the past with appropriate expressions of appreciation to the sponsoring church, the denomination, and others who have played an important part in bringing the new congregation to this historic moment. Even more important, the service should include an exciting look at the future with its challenges and opportunities. (See appendix, sample constitution service, p. 163.)

A new church has been born, has grown and developed over several years to a point of maturity, and is now on its own. A new "body of Christ" is now functioning in that place, an incarnation of the gospel, doing the work of Jesus as if He were there physically. Another "lighthouse for God" has been established in a dark place to beckon "whosoever will" to come and drink the water of life. And God's work goes marching on!

NOTE

1. For help in preparing a Constitution and Bylaws, see the pamphlet, "The Church Constitution and Bylaws Committee" (Nashville, Tenn.: The Sunday School Board of the Southern Baptist Convention, 1977). See also *A Guide to Religious Incorporations* (Samford University: The Center for the Study of Law and the Church.

10

FAMILY PLANNING

"And so were the churches established in the faith, and increased in number daily" (Acts 16:5).

When a young couple gets married they usually begin to think about family planning.

Not every couple wants to have a baby immediately and some not at all. But it is only natural for those who love and respect life to want to pass it on. Eventually, at least, they hope to have a child, maybe several, and the home somehow does not seem quite complete without children.

God has given all living things a natural instinct to reproduce. Without this instinct life on earth would cease and the planet would become a desolate wasteland.

There is a spiritual instinct that compels the church to reproduce itself and give birth to another. The heart of the church grieves when it sees needs unmet, people unreached, and areas around it becoming spiritual wastelands. We know a Bible-preaching, witnessing, ministering church is needed anywhere there are people. One church alone can never meet the spiritual needs of our world, or probably, even our community. Try as we may, there are yet certain people we have not reached. Perhaps its their race or ethnic background or perhaps they represent a socioeconomic status different from our own. Or perhaps the challenge is just too great and the numbers of people too many for the churches now existing to effectively reach and evangelize.

And then there is the sheer joy of having a baby! Certainly, there is much pain and agony in delivery. There are endless frustrations, disappointments, heartaches, and times of grief in raising a child and bringing it to adulthood. But, even so, the joy of birthing and raising a child is more than worth the price.

Yes, when a church sets about to multiply itself by birthing a new congregation, there is a price to be paid. There is the loss of faithful members who feel God's call to be part of the new congregation. These are usually people loved and needed in the mother church and their presence will be greatly missed.

There is the financial cost of budgeting much-needed funds to help the new work. This financial drain may continue for a number of years while the new church struggles to get established.

Also, there is a spiritual price to pay. Sometimes a new baby church proves a frustration. Like our own children, these new babies tend to become rebellious at times, maybe even defiant. Sometime they appear totally ungrateful, wanting to go their own way long before it is appropriate. Nevertheless, in spite of all these obstacles and difficulties, the fact remains that churches must be started if our nation and the world is to be evangelized and congregationalized as the Great Commission ordered. The happiest Christians in the world are members of a congregation that has given itself unselfishly to missions, generously supporting mission causes through their denomination's world missions programs, while at the same time being involved directly in missions by sponsoring new churches and ministries where needed. Happy indeed is the congregation that can proudly boast—and even show pictures—of their children and their children's children, churches populating a community as a result of their church planting efforts.

Many churches extend their arms hundreds of miles in many different directions. Southern Baptist churches in the South, where the work is strong and many of the churches are large, have found it advantageous to become partners with state conventions, associations, and local churches in the North, cosponsoring or assisting work where resources are scarce. At this moment, hundreds of Southern Baptist churches in the South are financially supporting new congregations throughout the North. In addition to their financial support, short-term mission groups such as lay-witnessing teams, missionary builders, youth and student groups to lead Vacation Bible Schools and backyard Bible clubs, evangelistic teams to conduct revivals, all these and many more journey northward to assist new congregations.

In 1991 over 56,000 Southern Baptists participated in volunteer short-term mission projects. In that same year over 250 new church buildings were built and approximately 100 were remodeled and renovated by missionary builders.

As a newly constituted church makes plans to start a new mission, or at least assist in the starting of a new work, what are some of the options?

"One a year" plan.—Numbers of churches have set a goal to start a new mission, or assist in beginning one, every year.

When the Parsons Baptist Church in Columbus, Ohio, was less than a year old, they voted to set as their goal the beginning of a new mission every year. Each year they enlisted some of their members to be the nucleus of a new church in the Columbus area. They started their first mission while they were still a mission themselves. By the time they were five years old, they had started four new missions as well as having developed their work from mission status to a strong church, averaging several hundred in attendance.

Delaware Valley Baptist Church in Willingboro, New Jersey, the first Southern Baptist church in the Greater Philadelphia area, started their first mission when they were less than a year old and continued starting new missions nearly every year for a decade. Many of the churches in the Philadelphia area were the children of this new congregation while they were still meeting in temporary quarters in a school building or later in a house on a dead-end street.

The "one more every four" plan.—Some churches, like most parents, may feel having a new baby every year is a wee bit extreme. When they think of "family planning," they think of a little more time between children to take care of the ones they already have.

Cecil Sims, executive director of the Northwest Baptist Convention, suggests the "one more every four" approach. The church sets as its goal starting or assisting in the start of at least one new mission every four years. This gives the new mission time to develop and grow and, hopefully, become self-sufficient. About the time the new congregation is ready to constitute, the church missions development committee is locating a place God would lead them to start yet another new work.

Certainly, if every church in the Southern Baptist Convention would set a goal to either sponsor or assist in the beginning of a new work every four years, it would revolutionize our denomination's church planting effort. We would go far beyond our Bold Mission Thrust goal of 50,000 congregations by the year 2000 and would easily reach the goal of 15,000 new churches planted during the decade of the 90s!

The "key church" plan.—Large churches that have experienced phenomenal growth, such as Saddleback Valley Community Church in California, or older churches with large memberships and resources, such as First Baptist Church, Dallas; First Baptist Church, Houston; and First Baptist Church, Arlington, Texas; have certainly demonstrated what a single church strongly committed to church planting can do.

First Baptist Houston is well on its way to starting or restarting one hundred churches in the Houston area by the year 2000. Already twenty-two are underway and four are planned within the next year. These twenty-two mission congregations average over two thousand in attendance. Harvey Kneisel is the minister of missions at this great church, coordinating their church planting effort. Pastor John Bisango has given forceful leadership to this church in his determination to fulfill his vision of one hundred new or revived congregations.

For over forty years First Baptist Dallas has sought to reach the Dallas metro area with mission congregations. They now are sponsoring thirty-one missions, many storefront-type congregations in the inner city or ethnic areas of Dallas. Ten language groups are represented in these mission congregations. One of these congregations, a Hispanic church known as Calvary Chapel, is averaging over three hundred in attendance. Shalom Fellowship, a messianic Jewish congregation, is sponsored by First Baptist Church and meets in their facilities. Last year these mission congregations averaged 2,400 in weekly attendance and baptized 582—half the baptisms reported by First Baptist Church.

Longtime senior pastor, W. A. Criswell, has led the church in this mission vision, ably assisted by Lanny Elmore, the minister of missions at First Baptist, Dallas.

Oak Cliff Baptist is another Dallas Church doing an outstanding job penetrating its community with mission congregations. In its ninety-seven year history, the church had never started a single mission. However, in 1986, when Aubrey Patterson came to the church as Minister of Missions, a study was done that discovered 3,200 people living in sixteen apartment complexes within a mile and a half of the church. Only 6 percent attended church anywhere. In addition, there were pockets of ethnic peoples— Koreans, Hispanics, as well as Anglos and Blacks, who were not being reached by any church.

After a time of mission study and prayer for the Lord's leadership, the church plunged in. Over the next four years the church started twenty-two mission congregations in southwest Dallas County.

Mission points at Oak Cliff include church type missions and "indigenous satellite units" (ISUs). (See appendix, pp. 172-73.) Two of the mission congregations have already constituted as churches.[1]

Briarlake Baptist Church in Atlanta, Georgia, is another strong church with a phenomenal church-starting record. This year the church is thirty-three years old and has sponsored or cosponsored thirty-two missions, many of them traditional church starts that have since become self-supporting, constituted churches. At the present time, a Chinese, an Arabic, and a Hispanic congregation meet in the Briarlake building along with the Anglo congregation. Attendance totals over thirteen hundred.

Graceland Baptist Church in New Albany, Indiana, is a marvelous example of a church growing by extension as well as by expansion. This great church, located across the river from Louisville, Kentucky, has forty-five mission congregations, most of them led by members of the church and directed by outreach director Dan Jenkins.

Some of the congregations are traditional church type missions that will eventually constitute as churches. Most are satellite units meeting in high-rise apartments and retirement centers. On a typical Sunday, the mother church will average 1,100 in Sunday School and 1,800 in worship. However, attendance in the mission congregations will likely exceed 1,000! Rev. Steve Marcum is pastor of this fine church.

The key church concept is certainly not new in the history of Christendom. Charles Haddon Spurgeon, pastor of the famed Metropolitan Baptist Tabernacle in London, England, led that great church to sponsor over two hundred mission congregations throughout the London area. In addition to these church-type mission congregations, Metropolitan Tabernacle sponsored over one thousand ''preaching stations'' throughout London and nearby areas. Spurgeon had weekly training sessions with the pastors of these missions, giving them personal guidance and instruction. He later led in the founding of Spurgeon's College, primarily as a training institution for these mission pastors.

The Home Mission Board of the Southern Baptist Convention has recently approved the key church concept as a major strategy for the 1990s. HMB representatives are seeking to enlist key churches throughout the nation who will commit themselves to start at least five new missions every year and, following the first year, to have at least five missions in operation at all times. Further, the key church will agree to make church planting a priority and will employ a minister of missions to coordinate the planting and development of new churches. HMB leaders hope to have at least one key church in every great metropolitan area of the nation, and perhaps several in some areas. In some instances, the Home Mission Board and the state conventions will assist in the salary of the minister of missions, on a phase-down, phase-out basis.

The cosponsor plan.—Some churches may reason there is no need for more churches in their immediate area but would be willing to be the cosponsor, along with a primary sponsor, of a new congregation in some other state or place. The cosponsor would contribute significant funding, which the primary sponsor may not be able to afford. The primary sponsor, because of its proximity to the new work, will give guidance and direction to the new congregation and may even provide several families as a nucleus. However, both the primary sponsor and the new congregation will look to the cosponsor for needed financial support and for other assistance that may be given by volunteer mission teams who visit the field.

The size may not be as important as the spirit in determining who might be a key church or a cosponsoring church. If it is mission-minded, earnestly desires to be part of the church planting task, and has the financial means to do so, a church could well be a cosponsor, giving at least $1,000 a month for several years to a new mission. They might even be a key church if they are willing to employ a minister of missions and commit themselves to the challenge of starting five new churches every year.

The assisting church.—The assisting church has been defined as "any church, anywhere, willing to give any amount, to help support directly a new mission congregation." Surely, even the smallest country church could respond to that kind of challenge. Even as little as $50 or $100 per month contributed to a new mission congregation involves the church in a new church start and will likely create a new spirit of excitement for and in support of missions in general.

Experience indicates the involvement of a church in the support of direct missions increases their overall missions support rather than deflecting from it. Perhaps one of the best ways to increase your church's gifts through the Cooperative Program and other missions support channels is to create the personal touch that results from direct involvement with a new congregation.

State missions directors of the forty-one state conventions and fellowships affiliated with the Southern Baptist Convention were requested to identify locations in their particular states where new work needs to be established immediately. When the information was gathered and tabulated, there were 22,000 potential sites throughout the United States, its territories, and Canada, where new congregations need to be established *now*! These potential locations were plotted on a map of the United States and published in *MissionsUSA* magazine. A copy of the map now hangs on the wall of the Home Mission Board's president's office in Atlanta, Georgia.

Truly, the field is white already unto harvest. "Say not ye, There are yet four months, and then cometh harvest? behold, I say unto you, Lift up your eyes, and look on the fields; for they are white already to harvest. And he that reapeth receiveth wages, and gathereth fruit unto life eternal: that both he that soweth and he that reapeth may rejoice together" (John 4:35-36).

If we wait the harvest will perish. Souls will be lost forever if we delay our church-planting task. Lord help us that even the new congregation will soon be making plans to start a new church where a mission is needed.

NOTE

1. *MissionsUSA*, February 1992.

11

FIRE FROM HEAVEN

"Now when Solomon had made an end of praying, the fire came down from heaven, and consumed the burnt offering and the sacrifices; and the glory of the Lord filled the house" (2 Chron. 7:1).

Everything seemed ready. The beautiful temple was complete. For months and years they had dreamed of the day when they would move into their new building. No effort had been spared to make it the most beautiful, commodious, attractive worship center in the land. It eclipsed all other shrines. Over 100,000 talents of gold and 1,000,000 talents of silver had contributed to its construction, equivalent to millions of dollars in today's currency. It took over seven years to build and over 30,000 carpenters, craftsmen, and artisans assisted in its construction. The entire interior was overlaid with gold and its walls were carved with cherubim, palm trees, and flowers. Indeed, it was a beautiful edifice!

But something was lacking! In spite of its beauty and grandeur, the presence of the Lord was not in that place. Beautiful ornate buildings with attractive decor are not sufficient. Without the presence of the Lord, nothing really matters.

As the people gathered to dedicate this great temple, Solomon began to pray. His prayer was long and fervent. The entire sixth chapter of 2 Chronicles recites his prayer as he called out to God for His blessing upon His people and the temple. As he concluded his prayer, "The fire came down from heaven, . . . and the glory of the Lord filled the house" (2 Chron. 7:1).

Have you ever been in a place of worship when the fire fell? When the "glory of the Lord filled the house?" A church cannot really function as the body of Christ in its community until the Spirit of the Lord is upon that congregation. Jesus said very simply, "Without me ye can do nothing" (John 15:5). Notice, He did not say without me you cannot do much or you cannot do many things very well. He was emphatic in His declaration of "without me ye can do *nothing*." Thus, it behooves the church of the Lord Jesus Christ to earnestly seek His face and pray for His blessing. The prayers of the church must not be perfunctory, simply a formality used to begin the service and conclude it. Jesus reminds us that the Father's house should be, above all else, "the house of prayer" (Matt. 21:13).

Nothing is more important to the church and its ability to minister than prayer. Prayer is more important than preaching, teaching, music, or anything else we ever do in God's house. Prayer and praise is the heartbeat in the life of any congregation.

Prayer During the Worship Services

Above all, the pastor of the new congregation should be a prayer leader. He must be sensitive to the needs of the congregation, praying individually and corporately for those needs.

It might be well to invite the congregation, led by the deacons, to come forward and kneel at the altar, while he or someone he designates leads the congregation in prayer. Those who lead in public prayer should be Spirit-filled prayer warriors, carefully chosen by the pastor because of their mighty power in praying. They should be people who pray with genuine concern and with a spirit of praise and thanksgiving for God's blessings.

Beware of calling on someone to lead in prayer without careful forethought. They may recite nice sounding words, but they will likely not lead the congregation to lay hold of the power of God.

Midweek Prayer Services

The so-called Wednesday evening prayer service is often anything but a prayer meeting. Ample time should be given at every midweek prayer service to list the needs of the congregation and bring them before the Lord.

It may be well to give everybody a prayer request slip as they enter the service on which they record any special prayer requests. While the congregation is singing an opening hymn, these may be collected and shared with the pastor.

At the appropriate moment, while the congregation is bowed in prayer, the pastor will slowly read these requests asking the members to pray for them even as they are mentioned. Again, it may be well if the leaders of the congregation along with any members that wish to join them, kneel at their seats or at the altar as these prayers are made.

Certainly, there is no magic in posture. But the Scripture does say, "If my people, which are called by my name, shall *humble themselves* and pray, and seek my face, and turn from their wicked ways, then will I hear from heaven, and will forgive their sin, and will heal their land" (2 Chron. 7:14, emphasis added). Certainly, God's people should never be ashamed to "humble themselves" as they pray, coming before the Lord on their knees.

The First Baptist Church, Dallas, Texas, has the largest membership of any Southern Baptist congregation and is probably also one of the wealthiest in the denomination. Yet, at every worship service and during every prayer time, the entire congregation goes to their knees in prayer! Kneelers have been installed on every pew, making it convenient and comfortable for this great congregation of several thousand to kneel every time they pray. Is it any wonder that God has so richly blessed this church through the years?

Prayer and Praise Meetings

In addition to the regular worship services and the midweek prayer service, some congregations have found it advantageous to have other meaningful prayer times as well. Some have weekly or even daily early morning prayer meetings where people assemble for prayer and praise on their way to work.

Others have found an occasional late-night or all-night prayer and praise meeting to be meaningful. Some churches frequently have all-night prayer meetings prior to a revival, evangelistic crusade, or other special event.

A Missouri church has prayer and praise meetings every Friday night at 10:00 p.m., often going until midnight and beyond. Although the number present is not great, those who attend are richly blessed. They often scatter through the sanctuary with a prayer warrior kneeling at every pew praying for those who will sit in that place the following Sunday. They pray that any in the building who are unsaved will come to Christ and everyone present will be blessed. Sometimes they gather around the pastor and the pulpit and pray that the Spirit of God will be upon him mightily as he proclaims the Word of the Lord. They share specific needs and pray for one another. Members of this church know these late-night prayer meetings have been the source of great power in the work and ministry of their church.

Personal Prayer and Anointing

In addition to corporate prayer experienced by the congregation when they gather for worship, every member, led by the pastor, should develop a meaningful prayer life of their own. Every Christian needs to start the day with a meaningful prayer time and a time in God's word. If not at the beginning of the day, certainly sometime through the day the Christian needs a quiet time with God. The church as a whole will likely not be a Spirit-filled congregation if the members individually do not daily seek His face. A meaningful prayer time is not an option, it is imperative if the church is to do its task effectively in the place where God has put it.

So the work of the Lord continues as He calls out His people, organizes them into an effective functioning body of Christ in the place where He has planted this new church, then leads that church to multiply itself by starting yet another. Thus, the Great Commission is being fulfilled and the Lord's work is being done even as He commanded, "unto the uttermost part of the earth" (Acts 1:8).

APPENDIX

Church Starting Planning Form

Target Area/Community _____

City/State _____ Association _____

Sponsoring Church _____

1. Population/

Demographics	1980	Current	1990	Projected 2000
Number	_____	_____	_____	_____
Percentage Increase	_____	_____	_____	_____

(Complete & attach an Area Analysis for Church Extension)

2. Preparation Plans/Actions (What will we do?)	Date (When?)	Responsibility (Who?)	Resources (Costs?)
Sponsoring-Church Leaders			
Sponsoring church committed	_____	_____	_____
Missions Development council selected	_____	_____	_____
_____	_____	_____	_____
Church Preparation			
Films/special services	_____	_____	_____
Missions presentations	_____	_____	_____
Series of messages	_____	_____	_____
Discipleship Training equipping centers	_____	_____	_____
Prayer emphasis	_____	_____	_____
Commitment service	_____	_____	_____
Start-a-Church Commitment Sunday	_____	_____	_____
_____	_____	_____	_____
Prospect Surveys			
Sample survey	_____	_____	_____
Telephone	_____	_____	_____
Door-to-door	_____	_____	_____
_____	_____	_____	_____
_____	_____	_____	_____
Cultivation Plans			
Complete surveys	_____	_____	_____
Regular visitation	_____	_____	_____
VBS/Backyard Bible Clubs	_____	_____	_____
Community activity	_____	_____	_____
_____	_____	_____	_____
_____	_____	_____	_____
Fellowship Period			
Leadership/curriculum	_____	_____	_____
Meeting places	_____	_____	_____
Joint fellowships	_____	_____	_____
_____	_____	_____	_____
_____	_____	_____	_____
New Church Launch			
Arrange meeting places/facilities	_____	_____	_____
Select relational guidelines	_____	_____	_____
Organize Sunday School/officers	_____	_____	_____
Plan worship service	_____	_____	_____
_____	_____	_____	_____
_____	_____	_____	_____

Total Cost (prior to launch):   _____

Church Starting Planning Form

(continued)

3. Church Planter/Mission Pastor/Contact Person

Name ______________________ Phone ____________

Address ______________________

City/State/Zip ______________________

4. Mission Plans and Goals

	At Launch	6 Months	First Year	Second Year
Sunday School Attendance				
Number of units (1-18)				
Number of workers (1-8)				
Sunday School Enrollment				
Worship Service Attendance				
Membership				
Baptisms				
Average Offerings				
Projected annual offerings				

5. Projected Budget Plans and Funding Sources

(Complete and attach a projected Church Budget Worksheet for first two years.)

Funding Sources (monthly amounts):

Need	Year	New Church	Sponsor	Partner	Assisting Churches 1	2	3	4	5	Association	State	HMB	Total
Mission Pastor Support Package													
	1992												
	1993												
	1994												
	1995												
Purchase Church Site													
	1992												
	1993												
	1994												
	1995												
Construct First Unit Building													
	1992												
	1993												
	1994												
	1995												
Special Projects													
1	1992												
2	1993												
3	1994												
4	1995												
Total Funds:													

Note: All figures are monthly amounts for calendar years. The sponsoring church (Sponsor) and the partnership church (Partner) are long-term commitments for the five years of the project. Assisting churches may make short or long-term commitments. The monthly total should be adequate to meet the attached Church Budget Worksheet projections.

Completed by ______________________ Date ____________

Area/Community Analysis For Church Extension

Associational Priority No. _____
State Priority No. _____

THIS ANALYSIS SHOULD BE MADE IN PREPARATION FOR NEW CHURCH EXTENSION

City	State	County

Area's Name (Description of area in adjacent map)

Association

Name of Associational Director of Missions

Name of Associational Missions Development Director

Name of Person Completing this Analysis

1. RELIGIOUS DATA
(Resource: Personal Interviews, Telephone Yellow Pages and Observation)

(1) How many unchurched are in this area?

Unchurched	Number	*Percent
Baptist preference		
Other preference		
Total		100%
Names and addresses in hand		/////
Have expressed interest		/////

*Percent is calculated by dividing the total into the number in each group

_____ Miles

Paste-up or sketch map of target area

(2) What percent of the people in the area attend religious services? Weekly Monthly Seldom Never

(3) Does any Southern Baptist church attempt to reach this area now? How? _____

(4) If previous attempts to start a church in this area failed, why? _____

(5) Nearest Southern Baptist church:

   1) How many miles is it from target community? 2) Is this church compatible with the kind of church that needs to be started in this area?

_____

(6) Southern Baptist churches logical to sponsor new work: _____

(7) Denominations represented in the area by name and membership:

	Number Members	Number Attendants	Number Churches		Number Members	Number Attendants	Number Churches
Southern Baptist				Episcopal			
Other Baptist				Methodist			
Catholic				Presbyterian			
Jewish				Lutheran			
Other non-evangelical				Assembly of God			
Other				Nazarene			

2. POPULATION DATA (Resource: 1990 Census and Planning Commission)

(1) What is the present population of the area by the ethnic and age groups listed below?

Ethnic/Cultural Groups			Age Groups		
Types	Number	Percent	By Years	Number	Percent
White			0-17 years		
Black			18-34 years		
Hispanic			35-54 years		
Asian			55-64 years		
European			65 and over		
Other			Total		

(2) Population	1970	1980	1990	2000 (Projected)

3. ECONOMIC DATA (Resource: Local office employment agency for state and planning commission)

(1) Describe the area economy (agriculture, manufacturing, mining, government installations and institutions, military, commerce and trade, tourism, recreation)

(2) What are the five largest job classifications represented in the area? (manufacturing, agriculture, construction, transportation, trade, finance, service, mining, and government)

1)   2)

3)   4)   5)

(3) What percentage of the people are in each of the following categories?

Employment Groups	Percent	Income Groups	Percent
Executive, administrative and managerial		Less than 10,000	
Professional specialty		10,000—14,999	
Health technologists and technicians		15,000—24,999	
Technologists and technicians, except health		25,000—34,999	
Sales occupations		35,000—49,000	
Clerical and administrative support occupations		50,000 and Over	
Service occupations			
Farming, forestry and fishing occupations		(4) Type of Community ☐ Inner City ☐ New Town ☐ Open Country ☐ Transitional	
Production and maintenance occupations		☐ Suburban ☐ Exurban (Rural Urban) ☐ Small Town ☐ City	

(5) What are the present housing trends in this area?

Occupancy	Number	Percent	Type Housing	Units	Percent
Owner			* Single family		
Renter			** Multifamily		
			Mobile home		
Total		100%	Total		100%

* 1 unit in structure   ** 2 or more units

(6) Educational attainment (%)	Elementary School	High School	Prof./Tech.	College	Graduate
	%	%	%	%	%

Church Budget Worksheet

Congregation's Name _____

Budget Items	Amount Budgeted
MISSIONS	
World Missions	
National Missions	
Local Missions	
STAFF SUPPORT	
Pastor's Salary	
Housing	
Travel	
Annuity	
Insurance	
Convention Expense	
Cleaning Coordinator	
Secretary	
Other	
MINISTRIES	
Sunday School	
Vacation Bible School	
Discipleship Training	
Music	
Youth	
Local Mission Units	
Revivals	
Pulpit Supply	
Literature	
Other	
BUILDING	
Payment	
Insurance	
Maintenance	
Cleaning Supplies	
Rent	
Utilities	
Other	
OFFICE EXPENSES	
Bulletins	
Equipment	
Postage	
Supplies	
Other	
TOTALS	

Sample Relationship Agreement

Good communication is the key to good relationships. The sponsoring church shall appoint a church Missions Development (CMD) council to work with the mission congregation's steering committee or council. It is the responsibility of the two councils to develop and maintain good communication between the sponsoring church and the mission congregation.

In reality, the mission congregation is the church. It is simply the church meeting in a different place. It is the church extended. The mission congregation shall be governed by the constitution of the sponsoring church in all matters that pertain to it.

1. Relationships
   (1) The mission congregation and the sponsoring church shall agree on the person to be called as pastor of the mission congregation.
       1) A committee of five—three members from the mission congregation and two members from the sponsoring church—shall be elected as a pulpit committee.
       2) The prospective pastor shall be asked to speak before both congregations and be voted on by both.
   (2) The mission-congregation pastor shall move his church membership to the sponsoring church.
   (3) The mission-congregation pastor and the sponsoring-church pastor shall agree on evangelists to invite for mission-congregation revivals.

2. Church Membership
   Mission-congregation members can be received according to membership provisions of the sponsoring church's constitution. After accepting a candidate's request for church membership, the mission congregation shall submit the candidate's name to the sponsoring church for vote and baptism or to obtain a church letter.

3. Business
   (1) Any ordinary business items related to the mission congregation's work may be transacted by the mission congregation. Business items that directly involve the sponsoring church should be presented to the sponsoring-church clerk one week prior to the church's monthly business meeting. In no case will the mission congregation become indebted without the sponsoring church's approval.
   (2) The mission congregation shall submit a written report of all mission-congregation business, attendance, and growth at the sponsoring church's monthly business meeting.
   (3) The mission congregation shall be in contact with the sponsoring CMD council on matters of business and meet with the council as needed for reports and other communication.
   (4) The mission congregation may observe the ordinances of the church upon approval of the sponsoring church.

4. Tithes and Offerings
   (1) All tithes and offerings shall be kept by a treasurer, elected by the mission congregation, and approved by the sponsoring church. The treasurer shall make a monthly report of all receipts and expenditures.

   (2) The mission congregation shall support world missions through the Cooperative Program.
   (3) The mission congregation shall designate a percentage to associational missions.
5. General
   (1) The mission congregation shall use the Bible as the basis of its teachings.
   (2) The mission congregation shall use Southern Baptist program materials.
   (3) When the sponsoring church and/or the mission congregation determines that the mission congregation is strong enough to organize into a New Testament church, they should express this to the CMD council. In business session, the CMD council should recommend, for church and mission congregation action, that the mission congregation constitute as a church.
   (4) The sponsoring church shall do all in its power to enable the mission congregation to be the church God intends it to be. Prayer for the mission congregation is essential. The church shall be available for spiritual guidance, counsel, and assistance in visitation. The mission congregation shall pray for, love, respect, and cooperate with the sponsoring church for the mutual blessings of both.

Sponsoring Church Name _____

Sponsoring Church Approval Date _____

Signed _____
                              (pastor/moderator/clerk)

Mission Congregation Name _____

Mission Congregation Approval Date _____

Signed _____
                              (pastor/moderator/clerk)

Monthly Report of Mission Congregation to Sponsor(s)

End-of-Month Date _____

Mission Congregation Name _____

ENROLLMENT: Sunday School (S.S.) _____ , Discipleship Training (D.T.) _____ ,
            Other _____.

ATTENDANCE:

Week Service Leader	Worship A.M.	P.M.	S.S.	D.T.	Other
1st					
2nd					
3rd					
4th					
5th					
TOTALS					
AVERAGES					

(Note: Indicate special events, dates, and attendance—revivals, study courses—on the back of this sheet.)

VISITS TO: Prospects _____   Members _____

MEMBERSHIP: Baptism   Letter
New-Member Applications:
Enclosed with this Report   _____   _____
Mailed   _____   _____
    Total   _____   _____

Resident Members (including new applicants) _____
Nonresident members _____
(On back of sheet, list names added this month for nonresident and/or deceased [with date of death] members.)

FINANCES:
Balance from last month $ _____

Local receipts:		Expenditures:	
1st Week	$ _____	Local	$ _____
2nd Week	_____	Associational	_____
3rd Week	_____	Cooperative Program	_____
4th Week	_____	Special	_____
5th Week	_____	Total Expenditures	_____
Subtotal	_____		
Special	_____		
Outside Offering	_____		
Total Receipts	$ _____	Balance on Hand	$ _____

REQUESTS TO SPONSORING CHURCH. *(Use back of sheet.)*
ITEMS FOR APPROVAL. *(Use back of sheet.)*

Signed _____
       Mission Congregation Pastor/Leader/Moderator/Clerk

Treasurer's Monthly Report for _____ 19_____

Congregation's Name _____

Treasurer _____

Budget Items	Amount Budgeted	Expenditures This Month	Budget Balance
MISSIONS			
Cooperative Program			
Associational Missions			
Local			
STAFF SUPPORT			
Pastor's Salary			
Housing			
Travel			
Annuity			
Insurance			
Convention Expense			
Cleaning Coordinator			
Secretary			
Other			
MINISTRIES			
Sunday School			
Vacation Bible School			
Discipleship Training			
Music			
Youth			
Woman's Missionary Union			
Brotherhood			
Revivals			
Pulpit Supply			
Literature			
Other			
BUILDING			
Payment			
Insurance			
Maintenance			
Cleaning Supplies			
Rent			
Utilities			
Other			

Treasurer's Monthly Report (continued)

Budget Items	Amount Budgeted	Expenditures This Month	Budget Balance
OFFICE EXPENSES			
Bulletins			
Equipment			
Postage			
Supplies			
Other			
TOTALS			

INCOME   **EXPENDITURES**

1st Week	$_____	$_____
2nd Week	$_____	$_____
3rd Week	$_____	$_____
4th Week	$_____	$_____
5th Week	$_____	$_____

SPECIAL OFFERINGS

_____	$_____	$_____
_____	$_____	$_____
_____	$_____	$_____

OUTSIDE INCOME

_____	$_____	$_____
_____	$_____	$_____

OTHER

_____	$_____	$_____
TOTAL INCOME	$_____	TOTAL EXPENDITURES $_____

INCOME SUMMARY   **EXPENDITURES SUMMARY**

INCOME SUMMARY		EXPENDITURES SUMMARY	
Balance on Hand	$_____	Budgeted Amount Spent	$_____
Local Offerings	$_____	Special Offerings	$_____
Special Offerings	$_____	Other	$_____
Outside Income	$_____		
Other	$_____		
TOTAL			

RECAP

INCOME	$_____	SAVINGS OR RESERVE	$_____
LESS			
EXPENDITURES	$_____	OTHER ACCOUNTS	$_____
NEW BALANCE	$_____	_____	$_____

(New-congregation treasurer should prepare three copies, one for sponsoring church, one for the new-congregation pastor, and one for filing.)

The Mission Fellowship Leader

1. Qualifications
   (1) A person of unquestioned dedication to Christ.
   (2) A Southern Baptist by conviction and practice.
   (3) An active member of a Southern Baptist church.
2. Relationships
   (1) Work in cooperation with the director of missions and the associational Missions Development (AMD) council.
   (2) Communicate with immediate supervisors, the church Missions Development (CMD) council and sponsoring-church pastor.
3. Actions
   (1) Receive training provided for mission fellowship leaders.
   (2) Become familiar with the assigned field.
   (3) Develop the mission fellowship.
   (4) Encourage the sponsoring church to elect a CMD council.
   (5) Work with the CMD council and pastor in matters related to the mission fellowship community.
   (6) Secure homes for prayer and Bible study meetings.
   (7) Conduct Bible study and prayer meetings in homes.
   (8) Coordinate the work of volunteers for the mission fellowship field.
   (9) Develop a complete survey of the field. Set up an active file listing names, addresses, and telephone numbers of the unchurched.
   (10) Visit unchurched people.
   (11) Visit prospects and report progress and needs to the sponsoring church.
   (12) Lead people to Christ.
   (13) Train people to work in the new mission. Give attention to volunteers' motivation and attitudes.
   (14) Prepare for the launch of the mission congregation.
   (15) Assist the sponsoring church in securing a pastor for the mission congregation.
4. When the mission is ready to call a pastor, the association may ask the mission fellowship leader to accept another mission assignment.

Sample Founder's Day Service

Hymn
Scripture Reading
Welcome and Recognition of Visitors
Introduction
Missions Development Council Statement
   (CMD council gives reasons a church is needed in the community.)
Sponsoring-Church Affirmation
   (The sponsoring-church pastor affirms the new church, assuring members of the sponsoring-church's support.)
Presentation of Mission Congregation
   (Presiding person presents people involved in the mission congregation and announces locations and times of the mission's regular meetings.)
Hymn
Special Music
Message
Invitation
   (Invite people to become members of the new mission.)
Reception and Fellowship

Sample Motion to Constitute

"*Whereas*, We believe there is a need for a Baptist church in this community, and

Whereas, After prayer, we believe we have found God's divine guidance, and

Whereas, We have consulted with fellow Christians and neighboring churches, and

Whereas, We have called a council to consider this matter, and the council has recommended we proceed with the constitution of the new church,

Resolved, That we enter into the organization of a Baptist church."

Sample Constitution Service

Hymn
Scripture Reading
Prayer
Reading of the Mission Congregation's History
Welcome and Guest Recognition
Statement of Meeting's Purpose
Recommendation to Constitute
   (The sponsoring church recommends that the mission congregation constitute.)
Vote to Constitute
   (Members of the new church vote. The church is born at this point.)
Adoption of Church Covenant
Adoption of Articles of Faith, Constitution, and Bylaws
Vote to Affiliate
   (Vote is unnecessary if the constitution states that the church is affiliated with the local association, state convention, and Southern Baptist Convention.)
Recognition of Charter Members
Election of Officers
   (A nominating committee should present names of moderator, clerk, pastor, teachers, and other officers.)
Sponsoring-Church Vote
   (Sponsor votes to recognize the new congregation as a constituted church.)
Special Music
Message or Charge to New Church
Invitation for New Members
Offering
Benediction
Right Hand of Fellowship to Members of the Newly Constituted Church
Fellowship Time

Sample Commissioning Service

Hymn	"Send the Light"
Prayer	
Welcome and Recognitions	
Hymn	"Set My Soul Afire"
Scripture	Romans 10:12-15 or Isaiah 6:1-13
Offering	
Mission Testimony	
Special Music	"People to People"
Message	
Invitation	

(Invite all who plan to work in or attend the mission congregation to come forward for dedicatory prayer and remain for congregational greetings.)

Responsive Reading	*(See sample below.)*
Dedicatory Prayer	
Hymns	"Tell the Good News"
	"Reach Out and Touch"

Closing Prayer

Sample Responsive Reading

Pastor: "Then I heard the voice of the Lord saying, 'Whom shall I send? And who will go for us?' And I said, 'Here am I. Send me!'"
(Isa. 6:8, NIV).

Congregation: "As it is written, 'How beautiful are the feet of those who bring good news!'" (Rom. 10:15, NIV).

Pastor: "Therefore go and make disciples of all nations, baptizing them in the name of the Father and of the Son and of the Holy Spirit, and teaching them to obey everything I have commanded you. And surely I am with you always, to the very end of the age" (Matt. 28:19-20, NIV).

Congregation: "But you will receive power when the Holy Spirit comes on you; and you will be my witnesses in Jerusalem, and in all Judea and Samaria, and to the ends of the earth" (Acts 1:8, NIV).

Pastor: "We are therefore Christ's ambassadors, as though God were making his appeal through us. We implore you on Christ's behalf: Be reconciled to God" (2 Cor. 5:20, NIV).

Congregation: "For this reason, since the day we heard about you, we have not stopped praying for you and asking God to fill you with the knowledge of his will through all spiritual wisdom and understanding" (Col. 1:9, NIV).

Pastor: "Do not be anxious about anything, but in everything, by prayer and petition, with thanksgiving, present your requests to God. And the peace of God, which transcends all understanding, will guard your hearts and your minds in Christ Jesus" (Phil. 4:6-7, NIV).

List of Free Materials for New SBC Congregation

Sunday School Board

The Sunday School Board provides the following free material to new churches:
- $50 conference center discount,
- $25 gift certificate for Bible study and administrative materials,
- Materials to guide in starting a media library,
- 25 *Baptist Hymnals*,
- Graded choir literature for 3 months,
- Stewardship promotional material,
- One Holman King James Version pew Bible,
- $100 worth of Discipleship Training materials,
- *Vacation Bible School Plan Book*,
- Personal call or visit by a Sunday School consultant,
- Copy of current Church Materials Catalog,
- $100 of selected literature for one quarter.

Request a Free Materials Offer Form from the Sunday School Board (MSN 177), 127 Ninth Ave., N., Nashville, TN 37234.

Woman's Missionary Union (WMU)

Contact the state WMU office for free material explaining age-group organizations:
- Mission Friends (birth through 5),
- Girls in Action (6-11 or Grades 1-6),
- Acteens (12-17),
- Baptist Young Women (18-34), and
- Baptist Women (35 and older).

Brotherhood Commission

The Brotherhood Commission will provide literature free for three months to new churches and missions. This material is available for:
- Lads (ages 6-9),
- Crusaders (ages 9-11),
- Pioneers (ages 12-14),
- High School Baptist Young Men (ages 15-17),
- Baptist Young Men (ages 18-34), and
- Baptist Men (ages 35 and up).

Contact Brotherhood Commission's Customer Service Center, 1 800 727-6466 for an order form, "Free Brotherhood Periodicals for New Churches and Missions."

Home Mission Board

Contact Home Mission Board Customer Services, 1 800 634-2462, for the following free items:

Guide for Planting Congregations (370-144F)
Guide for Growing New Churches (370-101F) limit 1
New Churches and New Converts (370-105F)
The New Church Growth Probe (370-106F)
Using Revivals to Start Churches (370-119F)
Constitution Packet (370-120F)
Starting Churches Through Revivals (370-125F)
Associational Church Extension Guide (370-127F)
The Bivocational Church Minister (370-32F)
Second Church/Another Church Start (370-63F)
Nine Steps in Starting New Churches (370-78F)
Why Do We Need New Churches Now? (370-87F)
The Church Evangelism Council Manual (220-21F)
A Word of Help for the Unsaved (223-86F)
Has Anyone Told You Today That Jesus Loves You? (223-111F)
An Invitation for You (223-93F)
Church/Community Needs Survey Guide (301-28F)
Guide for Establishing Ethnic Ministries and Congregations (350-33F)
Crossing Cultures to Start Churches (350-79F)

Sample Visitor Letter*

Dear _____._____,

It was a great joy to have you worship with us. We hope you enjoyed the services and will be with us often.

If you live in our area and are anxious to find a church home, let me urge you to consider our church. I believe we can be a blessing to your life, and you can be a blessing to us. We have a full program of activities designed to give you the best in spiritual training and Christian fellowship. This program inculdes Sunday School, Discipleship Training, Woman's Missionary Union, Brotherhood, Royal Ambassadors, Girls in Action, Acteens, and a complete music program. Our youth and recreation programs are considered by many to be outstanding.

May the Lord bless you in your service to Him. If I can ever be of any help to you, don't hesitate to let me know.

[*sent to all visitors in worship services]

Sample New Member Letter

Dear _____,

We want to take this opportunity to welcome you into our church family and wish the blessings of the Lord upon your life as we serve Him together. We trust that your stay here will be a long, fruitful, and happy one and that we will be a blessing to one another and to our Lord.

I invite you to attend our New Members Class which meets weekly, Sunday evenings at 6:00 p.m. The class includes four sessions designed to instruct you concerning the meaning of church membership, the history and doctrines of Baptists, and the nature of our church. You can begin attending the class any Sunday. My wife and I conduct the class, which meets in the church fellowship hall.

Follow-Up Program

Delaware Valley Baptist Church

1. As inquirer comes forward, he is met by pastor who discerns his need, then introduces him to a deacon. (Deacons come forward at beginning of invitation and stand at the front row.)
2. Deacon counsels with inquirer from the Bible, then kneels with him and leads him in prayer ("sinners prayer" if lost; "backsliders prayer" if on rededication; prayer of thanks if moving membership; etc.)
3. Deacon fills out triplicate decision card on inquirer. (Tears off top copy and gives to pastor; others are picked up by clerk and secretary.)
4. Deacon gives Bible study packet to new Christian, explains the materials, and gets him started on lesson 1.
5. The person is introduced to the congregation and Sunday School teacher stands with him.
6. Members greet inquirer. Organization leaders are to invite new member to their meetings.
7. On Monday, a member is assigned to the new member as sponsor and is sent a letter and report cards. They are to visit in their home, invite them to their own home for a snack or meal, and be a real friend.
8. A deacon visits the new member, gives them a new members packet, goes over the materials, etc.
9. The pastor and his wife visit the new member, outline the formula for spiritual growth, help him get started on a Bible study program, and fill out a Christian Service Survey card.
10. Sunday School teacher visits the new member and strives to enroll him or her in Bible teaching if not already enrolled.
11. New member letter is sent to the new member, welcoming him or her into the church fellowship and inviting him or her to the "New Members' Fellowship."
12. New member attends "New Members' Class" meeting during Discipleship Training on Sunday evenings.
13. "New Members' Fellowship" after church the first Sunday of every month; members meet new members; baptismal certificates distributed.
14. Every Monday and Tuesday pastor visits members, especially those who have missed several Sundays.
15. Every week pastor goes through church roll and calls members who might need a contact.
16. Sunday School teachers are expected to call or visit members immediately if absent.
17. New member is assigned to a deacon-sponsor. Deacons visit at least one member/family a week and any member in time of crisis (death, sickness, etc.).

Sample Letter of Invitation to
Sister Churches for a Constitution Service

Dear Pastor:

The _____ Baptist Congregation, a mission of the _____ Baptist Church, desires to constitute as a duly organized New Testament church to be affiliated with the _____ Baptist Association, the _____ State Convention, and the Southern Baptist Convention. We invite you and your members to be present for the constitution service Sunday afternoon, _____ _____ (date and time). Pastors should be present at _____ (time) to form an examining council.

On _____ (date), the _____ Baptist Church voted unanimously to approve the intent of this mission to constitute as a church.

Respectfully,

Larry Lewis, Pastor

enclosure: Proposed constitution and bylaws

STEPS IN A BUILDING PROJECT

Survey Phase

I. Identify property and building inadequacies
1. List general inadequacies
2. Review list of inadequacies with key program leaders

II. Secure outside help
1. Request help from Church Building Consultant in state office and/or Church Architecture Department
2. Obtain *Church Property/Building Guidebook* from Baptist Book Store
3. Study chapters 1, 2, and 3 in guidebook for help in organizing a committee and conducting a building project

III. Secure church action to appoint a Survey, Planning and Building Committee
1. Report property and building inadequacies to the church
2. Ask for approval to structure a Survey, Planning and Building Committee to begin a study that is directed at the church taking actions to meet property and building needs

IV. Organize and train committee
1. Elect building project steering committee
2. Appoint three to five or more members on each subcommittee
3. Train committee using *Church Property/Building Guidebook* for textbook

V. Explore community needs to discover church opportunities
1. Survey community
2. Determine specific needs of persons in the community
3. Brainstorm church's mission
4. Determine number of persons who might be reached in each program

VI. Develop a comprehensive program
1. Define and prepare a written statement of programs to be provided by the church
2. Ascertain number of people for which space will be provided in each church program

VII. Evaluate suitability and adequacy of church site
1. Evaluate location
2. Determine amount of property needed

VIII. Prepare financial plan
1. Review past and present financial performance
2. Make initial contact with Stewardship Commission, or other sources of help regarding a fund-raising campaign
3. Project amount of money to be raised in an intensive fund-raising campaign
4. Investigate sources for borrowing funds, and potential amounts available
5. Secure tentative loan commitments from selected mortgagee
6. Determine maximum funds which can be made available for a building project

Planning Phase

IX. Prepare property use plot and floor plans
1. Obtain accurate floor plans of existing building
2. Identify uses of present space and any temporary space being used
3. Examine structural condition of building(s) to identify any needing replacing
4. Determine amount and type of new space needed
5. Acquire an accurate plot plan of church's property including any to be acquired
6. Forward all program information, property plans, and floor plans to Church Architecture Department for preparation of preliminary plot plan and floor plans. (Forms are available from the Church Architecture Department for assembling information needed by the department.)
7. Evalute Church Architecture Department plans

X. Report to church and secure church decision

1. Report findings and recommendations to church
   (1) Program needs for which space will be provided
   (2) The proposed site development plans and floor plans for immediate space to be constructed
   (3) Anticipate cost of immediate building project
   (4) Means and source of financing project
   (5) Growth and other results anticipated from the building project
2. Secure church action on
   (1) Type and amount of space to be constructed
   (2) Acquisition of any properties needed
   (3) Employment of architect, and going ahead with securing construction drawings on basis of cost estimates
   (4) The plan for financing the project

XI. Secure preliminary and design drawings for project and simultaneously begin fund raising campaign

1. Instruct architect to prepare floor plans and cost estimates following church's approval on type and amount of space to be provided
2. Begin the fund raising campaign
3. Present plans and cost estimate to church for approval
4. Instruct architect to prepare design development plans including materials and finishes, and prepare revised cost estimates
5. Review drawings and present the plans and cost estimate to church for approval

XII. Secure construction drawings

1. Instruct architect to proceed with preparation of construction drawings in line with approved design development plans
2. Give church progress report when plans are completed and approved by the steering committee
   NOTE: Some of the actions of XI and XII are subject to being repeated if committee and/or church is not satisfied with work done by the architect

XIII. Begin organizational enlargement and leadership training simultaneously with beginning construction

1. Enlist new workers for enlarged organization
2. Inaugurate an aggressive and intensive training program for present and new workers
3. Design a "saturation" visitation program to be implemented immediately prior to occupancy of the new building

XIV. Select contractor, award contract and complete building construction

1. With architect's guidance select contractors from whom bids will be received
2. Furnish contractors with plans for project, including list of any alternates, and specify date bids are due
3. Receive bids, open and review with architect
4. Arrange for permanent financing, and secure the construction loan
5. Award contract to selected contractors, and notify other contractors of rejection of their bids
6. Secure bonding, and workman's compensation insurance
7. Order the furnishings needed
8. Inspect project periodically with architect and authorize payments to contractor at appropriate times
9. Make final inspection
10. Approve and accept work after contractor has completed all work according to contract agreements and plan specifications
11. Make final payment to contractor and architect

XV. Complete financing for building project

1. Make final arrangement with loan company for permanent financing
2. Set up in budget amount needed to make payments on loan
3. Secure appropriate insurance on the new building

XVI. Furnish and occupy building

1. Inspect furniture upon delivery
2. Install furniture after building is completed, and the building is heated or cooled as appropriate
3. Plan for entering new building with high attendance and new organization functioning at top efficiency
4. Plan service for dedication of building at appropriate time

Construction Phase

Determining Space in Age Division Rooms

Organization and Space Needs for Division Grouping and Grading

Division	Age	For Each Department		For Each Class		Suggested Floor Space Per Person			
						Department Room		Classroom	
		Maximum Enrollment	Anticipated Attendance Capacity[a]	Maximum Enrollment	Anticipated Attendance Capacity[a]	Minimum[b]	Recommended	Minimum	Recommended
Preschool	B-1	12	9	Not applicable		20 sq. ft.	35 sq. ft.[c]	None	None
	Toddlers	12	9						
	2	15	12			No Preschool room smaller than 12 × 16[d]			
	3	20	16						
	4	20	16						
	5	20	16						
Children	6-8	30	24	Not applicable[e]		20 sq. ft. 20×24[d]	25 sq. ft. 25×30[d]	None	None
	9-11[e]								
Youth	12-17	60	28-42	15	7-10	8 sq. ft.[f]	10 sq. ft.[f]	10 sq. ft.[f]	12 sq. ft.[f]
Adult	18-up	125	56-81	25	12-16	8 sq. ft.	10 sq. ft.	10 sq. ft.	12 sq. ft.

Space is provided for each person expected to be in the rooms of the building. Determining the number for which to plan is the result of a careful analysis of projected enrollment, organization, and attendance.

In determining the total number of square feet of educational space required, the church should add to the floor space mentioned above enough space for offices, corridors, stairways, rest rooms, storage, service space, and other accessory areas. This will require a total square footage of from 35 to 50 square feet per person in the educational building. Many churches should and will provide even more space.

(a) Average attendance may range from 45% to 70% of enrollment, depending on the age group and/or the community involved. Preschool and Children's workers recommend that space be provided on the basis of 80% of enrollment for these age groups. Youth and Adult workers recommend that space be provided on the basis of 70% of the enrollment.

(b) Minimum space footage may sometimes be necessary in smaller churches, first units, and mission buildings.

(c) Thirty-five square feet is considered as ideal. This amount and more may be required in churches planning to provide day care and kindergarten programs.

(d) For rationale on suggested minimum sizes and ratios, consult the Basic Program Books for the respective age divisions.

(e) Existing assemblies with classrooms may be used by departments in the Children's Division. Provide additional tables, chairs, and chalkboards as needed.

(f) If open room space is planned for Youth, department and classroom areas should be combined; 18-22 square feet per person.

Church Architecture Department, The Sunday School Board of the Southern Baptist Convention, Nashville, Tennessee

How to Start a New Indigenous Satellite Unit (ISU)

Bill McMullin left the insurance business to become Minister of Missions at the South Main Baptist Church in Pasadena, Texas, a suburb of Houston. He became the pastor of their first ISU (indigenous satellite unit) and has led in starting thirteen ISUs! Although three did not survive, the church is now sponsoring twelve satellite units and several others are planned. Several are Anglo congregations, but over half are Hispanic and African American. All the pastors are bivocational, but they are paid a minimal stipend by the church. These twelve satellite congregations average a total attendance of 200-225, about twenty each. Attendance at South Main Baptist Church averages 512 plus the ISUs for a total of more than seven hundred.

The majority meet in the community rooms of apartment buildings and some in mobile homes. The church sponsors an annual recognition service for their "mission ministries." They emphasize the direct involvement of their members in satellite ministries rather than mission trips and out of state projects. They call this "home cooking."

Bill McMullin lists several steps in starting a new indigenous satellite unit:

1. Pray for God's leadership and blessing.
2. Probe—"drive by" survey. Three most important factors are "location, location, location." Look for "pockets of people." The reasons churches die is they don't minister to the people around them.
3. Contact apartment managers. See if you can use the community room. If not, could you use an apartment? (They usually give the community room free; sometimes they may furnish an apartment for the pastor.)
4. Find a pastor-leader. Very important! Pick someone who can and will identify with the people. "Throw a hook out and see if he takes the bait. Drive by and look at the field. Also, talk to the wife and be sure she is supportive. Be willing to take a 'risk' —take a chance!"
5. Find "core group."
6. Launch the new work:
   Seven steps:
   (1) Have a printed flyer (mention casual dress, mention coffee and donuts).

(2) Provide folding chairs and other needed equipment.

(3) Provide $50.00 for a cultivation event (i.e. party, meal, rally, etc.).

(4) Do a survey, usually a Saturday morning before the first meeting (about five questions on a single form).

(5) Provide material for Bible study.

(6) Support your pastor-leader. Train him but don't "spoon-feed" him.

(7) Salary your pastor-leader—perhaps $125.00 for three months; $100 for two months; $50 for one month.

(8) Have annual recognition service for mission pastors (i.e. recognition banquet, recognition service, etc.).

BIBLIOGRAPHY

Amberson, Talmadge R., ed. *The Birth of Churches: A Biblical Base for Church Planting*. Nashville, Tenn.: Broadman Press, 1979.

Anderton, T. Lee. *Church Property Building Guidebook*. Nashville, Tenn.: Convention Press, 1980.

Arn, Win and Charles. *The Masters' Plan For Making Disciples*. Church Growth, 2670 S. Myrtle Avenue, Suite 201, Monrovia, Calif. 91016.

Barna, George. *The Frog in the Kettle: What Christians Need to Know About Life in the Year 2000*. Ventura, Calif.: Regal Books, 1990.

————. *User Friendly Churches: What Christians Need to Know About the Churches People Love to Go to*. Ventura, Calif.: Regal Books, 1991.

Bosch, David J. *Transforming Mission*. Maryknoll, New York: Orbis Books, 1991.

Brock, Charles. *The Principles and Practice of Indigenous Church Planting*. Nashville, Tenn.: Broadman Press, 1981.

Bunch, David, Harvey Kneisel, and Barbara L. Oden. *Multihousing Congregations: How to Start and Grow Christian Congregations in Multihousing Communities*. Atlanta, Ga.: Smith Publishing.

Chaney, Charles H. *Church Planting at the End of the Twentieth Century*. Wheaton, Ill.: Tyndale House, 1982.

Cho, Paul Yonggi. *Successful Home Cell Groups*. Plainsfield, N. J.: Logos International, 1981.

Crowder, Rowland E. *Designing Church Buildings for Southern Baptist Churches*. Nashville, Tenn.: Convention Press, 1976.

Currin, James. *Starting New Missions and Churches*. Nashville, Tenn.: The Baptist Sunday School Board, 1971.

Dayton, Edward R. and David A. Fraser. *Planning Strategies for World Evangelization*. Rev. ed. Grand Rapids, Mich.: William B. Eerdmans Publishing Co. and MARC, Monrovia, California, 1990.

Edge, Findley B. *A Quest for Vitality in Religion*. Nashville, Tenn.: Broadman Press, 1963.

Feeney, James II. *Church Planting by the Team Method*. Abbott Loop Christian Center, 2626 Abbott Road, Anchorage, Alaska 99507.

Fowler, Harry H. *Breaking Barriers of New Church Growth*. Creative Growth Dynamics, 129 Gulftide Court, Rocky Mount, North Carolina.

Graham, J.B. "Associational Missions Development," Home Mission Board, 1350 Spring Street, NW, Atlanta, Georgia 30367.

————. "Church Missions Development," Home Mission Board, 1350 Spring Street, NW, Atlanta, Georgia 30367.

Guide For Planting Churches. Atlanta, Georgia: Home Mission Board, New Church Extension Division, 1991.

Hadaway, C. Kirk. *Church Growth Principles: Separating Fact from Fiction*. Nashville, Tenn.: Broadman Press, 1991.

Hadaway, C. Kirk, Stuart A. Wright, and Francis M. DuBose. *Home Cell Groups and House Churches*. Nashville, Tenn.: Broadman Press, 1987.

Hodges, Melvin L. *A Guide to Church Planting*. Chicago, Ill.: Moody Press, 1973.

Hunter, George G. *Spread the Power: Church Growth in the Wesleyan Spirit*. Nashville, Tenn.: Abingdon Press, 1987.

Jones, Ezra Earl. *Strategies for New Churches*. New York: Harper & Row, 1976.

Kotter, John P. *Power and Influence*. New York: Free Press, 1985.

Lewis, Larry L. *Organize to Evangelize*. Nashville, Tenn.: Broadman Press, 1988.

Maston, T. B. *God's Will And Your Life*. Nashville, Tenn.: Broadman Press, 1964.

McCormick, Gwenn E. *Designing Worship Centers*. Nashville, Tenn.: Convention Press, 1988.

McCarty, Doran. *Leading the Small Church*. Nashville, Tenn.: Broadman Press, 1991.

McGavran, Donald A. and George Hunter III. *Church Growth Strategies That Work*. Nashville, Tenn.: Abingdon Press, 1980.

McNamara, Roger N. *A Practical Guide to Church Planting*.

Miller, Calvin. *Leadership*. Colorado Springs, Col.: NavPress, 1987.

Montgomer, Jim. *Dawn 2000: 7 Million Churches to Go*. Pasadena, Calif.: William Carey Library, 1989.

Murren, Doug. *The Baby Boomerang: Catching Baby Boomers as They Return to Church*. Ventura, Calif.: Regal Books, 1990.

Nee, Watchman. *The Normal Christian Church Life*. Washington, D.C.: International Students Press, 1969. Rev. Ed.

Neighbor, Ralph. *Where Do We Go from Here?* Houston, Tex.: Touch Outreach Ministries, 1991.

Neuhauser, Peg C. *Tribal Warfare in Organizations*. Cambridge, Mass.: Ballinger Publishing Co., 1988.

Perkins, Ernie. *Guidelines for the Pioneer Pastor*. Fairborn, Ohio: Encounter Publishing Co., 1971.

Redford, Jack. *Planting New Churches*. Nashville, Tenn.: Broadman Press, 1978.

Ro, Bong-Rin and Marlin L. Nelson. *Korean Church Growth Explosion*. Seoul, Korea: Word of Life Press and Asia Theological Association, Taiwan, 1983.

Robb, John D. *Focus: The Power of People Group Thinkers*. Monrovia, Calif.: MARC, 1989.

Robinson, Darrell W. *Total Church Life*. Rev. ed. Nashville, Tenn.: Broadman Press, 1991.

Schaller, Lyle E. *44 Questions for Church Planters*. Nashville, Tenn.: Abingdon Press, 1991.

Stacker, Joe R. and Bruce Grubbs. *Pastoral Leadership Skills*. Nashville, Tenn.: Convention Press, 1988.

Starr, Timothy. *Church Planting*. Willowdale, Ontario, Canada: Fellowship of Evangelical Baptist Churches, 1987.

Tidsworth, Floyd Jr. *Planting and Growing Missions*. Durham, N. C.: Moore Publishing Co., 1979.

Tinsley, William C. *Upon This Rock*. Atlanta, Ga.: Home Mission Board, 1985.

Thompson, W. Oscar, Jr. *Concentric Circles of Concern*. Nashville, Tenn.: Broadman Press, 1981.

Towns, Elmer. *Getting a Church Started*. Church Growth Institute, Box 4404, Lynchburg, Virginia 24502.

Towns, Elmer. *10 of Today's Most Innovative Churches*. Ventura, Calif.: Regal Books, 1991.

Wagner, C. Peter. *Church Planting for a Greater Harvest*. Ventura, Calif.: Regal Books, 1990.